BUSINESS
in GOD

BUSINESS in GOD

ERASE THE LINE BETWEEN
GOD'S WORK AND MAN'S WORK

BRYAN WATERS

DESTINY IMAGE™ EUROPE srl
Via Maiella, 1
66020 San Giovanni Teatino (Ch) - Italy

"Changing the world, one book at a time."

This book and all other Destiny Image™ Europe books are available at Christian bookstores and distributors worldwide.

To order products, or for any other correspondence:

DESTINY IMAGE™ EUROPE srl
Via della Scafa 29/14
65013 Città Sant'Angelo (Pe), Italy
Tel. +39 085 4716623 • +39 085 8670146
Email: info@eurodestinyimage.com
Or reach us on the Internet: www.eurodestinyimage.com

ISBN: 978-88-96727-24-9
For Worldwide Distribution, Printed in Italy.
1 2 3 4 5/14 13 12 11

DEDICATION

This book is dedicated to my best friend, the Holy Spirit, and to all those many brothers and sisters in the Lord who under His leading have impacted my life in one way or another.

ACKNOWLEDGMENTS

I delight to acknowledge my dear friends and supporters, Trevor and Cynthia Hollingsworth, who have encouraged me throughout this project, and especially Cynthia for her hours of work editing the manuscript. She is a true co-worker in the Lord.

My Pastor Taran and all my friends in Solomon's Porch fellowship.

My family and business colleagues who have always been ready to help.

Endorsements

In these times of financial turmoil, it is imperative that believers grasp the biblical principles which set a Christian approach to business apart from a non-Christian approach. In this fascinating and challenging book, Bryan shows a biblical perspective of business and profit-making which is hugely helpful.

Tony Cummings, published author,
international speaker, and music editor,
Cross Rhythms, UK

This is a must-read book.

Bryan has a truly amazing and unique way of explaining biblical truths and spiritual principals. Many of today's Christians work full-time for the church, and it's true that's what God wants. But when Bryan writes about his life's experiences and the biblical understanding of work and ministry, you begin to realize the plan God has and His vital need for all born-again believers to make a big difference in our societies today.

Bryan's practical insights into such things as spiritual momentum, discipline that leads to freedom, and starting a business are truly life-changing.

This wonderful teaching has impacted and changed many lives in Africa.

John A. Benson
Senior events manager
Lifeline Ministries, Uganda

This book goes a long way to dispel the myth that ministry for God is only for the chosen few within the walls of the church, and it uses many scriptural arguments to make the direct connection between business in the marketplace and the Kingdom of God. The author purposefully sets out, in a clear and easy-reading style, to empower the reader with the right foundation and skills to be successful for God. A unique and valuable contribution in Christian literature today, this book is a must for anyone either already in business or considering starting a new enterprise.

M.R.J. Pike
Author of *Defenders of Barracrail*
nominated Best Christian Book Award 2008
Founder and co director of Time Out Mission International

CONTENTS

PREFACE

There is a perception that work and business are secular, non-spiritual activities. I believe this view is held by a high proportion of the worldwide Church. This endemic culture cultivates a misplaced belief that to serve God properly one needs to become a member of the clergy, a missionary, or a similar full-time worker for God. This prevailing attitude is robbing the Church, keeping it materially poor and of little influence in the marketplace of society. It also induces and encourages poverty among the individuals and families in our churches.

I organize and speak at Business in God conferences, and I have written this book to play my part in addressing this misconception and to empower and encourage, in the light of God's Word, all those in the Church who work, whether it be for a church, a boss, as a student, a homemaker, an unpaid charity worker, or as a business owner.

I shall not only be establishing that work is a spiritual activity, but that it is also a ministry to the Lord and that God wants to and will work with us in our work; furthermore, our work is God's secret weapon for fulfilling the Great Commission and for improving the low moral and ethical values that are currently prevailing in society.

I have been amazed that in some countries where I have ministered I have heard that the church leaders have stated from the pulpit that people in the church had to choose between their business and the church. I have also observed that it is quite common in Africa for people to give up their work as soon as they are saved, because the prevailing ethos of their church is that work is not spiritual but secular. They will actually give up their jobs and attempt to do what they consider to be spiritual activities, like praying, praising, or just having fellowship. Meanwhile, their church remains poor and will get poorer as time goes by. In a continent with such potential to be self-sufficient in food production, where so many are starving and malnourished, the Church could and should be taking the lead by bringing God's blessing of food to the needy.

I believe God's plan is that the 99 percent of church attendees who are not on the staff of the church be taught and encouraged to become a mighty army for God in the workplace, allowing Him to transfer great wealth, power, and influence to the Church through them and cause the true Gospel to break out into and reside in every stratum of society.

How do we as a Church move forward into this vision? How do you eat an elephant? A bite at a time! I believe our first bite must be to receive a truly biblical revelation of the activity of work and to see work from God's viewpoint. This, by God's grace, I pray will happen for you as you read on.

INTRODUCTION

I have written this book for all those people who, like me, want to enter more fully into their destiny in God and aspire to rise like eagles on the thermals of the ways of God and who long to be eagles dwelling in high places. My hope and prayer is that by the time you have finished reading it you will have been made fully aware that, whoever and wherever you are, if you are a Christian, you are in full-time ministry for the Lord Jesus. Also, you will see that spirituality is not an activity but a position, a state of being. If you are truly spiritual, then what you do becomes spiritual, too.

Eagles

A young boy went for a walk up into the mountains of Scotland one day. As he scrambled over the rocks, he came across an eagle's nest with eggs in it. He took one, put it safely into his pocket, and set off down the mountain to his home. When he got home, he wondered what to do with the eagle's egg. He decided to put it into the nesting box of his mother's chicken pen. Sure enough, a brooding hen came along and looked at the egg, liked the look of it, and sat on it as though it were her own.

A few weeks later, the baby eagle emerged from the egg, saw all the chickens clucking away, scratching in the dirt, and assumed he was a chicken. He quickly joined in and copied everything the chickens did. They scratched the dirt so he scratched the dirt; they clucked so he clucked; they didn't fly so he didn't fly. They walked and ran around in circles a lot, so he walked and ran around in circles a lot.

There were times, however, when he would look up at the big white-topped mountain in the distance. He felt a deep longing inside and would say to himself, "How wonderful it would be to be able to fly to the top of that mountain!" Then he would look at the dirt at his feet and at his fellow chickens and shrug his feathers and say, "But I am only a chicken." He grew bigger and bigger and was otherwise content with his chicken life, scratching around in the dirt, clucking as he walked and ran around in circles.

But there came a day (there always comes a day for each one of us) when he looked up and saw a mighty eagle soaring above the chicken pen. He had never seen one so close before; it was as though he was almost inviting the chickens to join him. "Wait a minute," he said, looking at the eagle and then looking down at himself, "I look more like that eagle than I do the chickens." He ran over to the water trough to get a glimpse of himself in the water. "I am sure I look more like an eagle than these chickens. I am going to try flapping my wings and see what happens."

So he started flapping gently at first, feeling very embarrassed, because all the chickens were staring at him and starting to laugh, saying, "What are you doing, chicken? Trying to fly? Ha, ha, ha, how ridiculous!"

But as he flapped his wings, he rose a good two feet off the ground. "Wow!" he said, "Did you see that? I'll try again, much harder this time." And so he did, and before he knew it he was up in the air above the chicken pen. He shouted, "I am flying! I am an eagle, not a chicken! Wheeee! Whooo!"

As he rose higher and higher into the air, he was amazed at how very small that chicken pen was; it used to be his whole world, but now it seemed so small and insignificant. He had such good eyesight that he could see for miles and miles all around him. He flew higher and higher, right up to the top of that mountain. The air was so sweet and pure up there, and it was so peaceful and quiet—no clucking, no running around in circles. He saw the beauty of the crystal clear rivers and streams as they cascaded down the mountain, all singing different songs but all in perfect harmony, and the many and varied little flowers of different shapes and colors. They seemed to carpet whole areas of the mountain slopes. It was so good being an eagle and not a chicken!

Working for the Lord

As we continue in this book, we shall be looking at fundamental spiritual principles that are meant to govern our life attitudes and bring us into a deeper spiritual life and enable us to align ourselves with our destiny and live like eagles rather than like chickens scratching in the dirt. I believe that you will receive the revelation that God is a worker; God loves work, God is always working, and He has made you in His image—you are just like Him, designed and equipped to work, to be creative and rejoice in it. He has made you a mini-creator, and since God is a successful worker, he has made you to be a successful worker also.

His Word, His power, and all the resources of the heavenly Kingdom are geared to help you to be successful. God has a vision and plan for you, which is for you to be a success in every area of your life as you work.

Some of these principles can be seen in operation during the first 30 years of the life of Jesus Christ the Son of God. Like many of us, He grew up from babyhood and became a student, an apprentice, an employee, and finally a businessman running a carpentry business. During that time, He was still as much the Son of God as He was when He was engaged in His public ministry. What's more, God the Father was as pleased with Him during this time of His life as He was during the latter part of it.

We see an outward sign of the Father's approval at the time of Jesus' baptism by John the Baptist, prior to the start of His public ministry. God the Father spoke from Heaven and said, "This is My beloved Son, in whom I am well pleased" (Matt. 3:17). God the Holy Spirit agreed by descending on Jesus in the form of a dove. Until then, Jesus had only been a worker, but God was well pleased with Him. "Well pleased" means totally pleased with Him and His work. In fact, we could say that if Jesus had failed in the slightest way in the former part of His life the success of the latter part would not have been possible. The former was the foundation for the latter; the same is true for us, and there are no short cuts. God is a master builder and you are his project, and He is determined to change you from one degree of glory to another until you are just like Christ. There is only one way, and that is up if we cooperate with the Father in Christ Jesus.

Over the years as I have preached the contents of this book; I have seen people's lives change in remarkable ways. I have witnessed them move into a new hope, freedom, vision, and purpose.

I remember, during a conference in Volvograd, Russia around 2005, an old, peasant mother came forward for prayer. I forget her name but will call her Tischa (it seems to be the name the Holy Spirit is giving me for her now). Tischa had tears in her eyes as she walked up to me. I could see that she must have spent most of her life working outdoors on the land, because her skin was well weathered, having the texture and color of brown leather. Her furrowed brow betrayed the fact that she must have had a very hardworking life, probably one like so many peasant subsistence smallholders, farming their family land, trying to eke out a living for their households. This was confirmed as she stretched out her hands to me and I took hold of them. They were manual labor type working hands, used to holding farming implements in all kinds of weather, hard and tough.

She spoke quietly to me via an interpreter as she sobbed, "Thank you, thank you for showing me that all those years of hard work for what seemed so little return are valuable and acceptable to Jesus. I thought they were wasted years without God. As we prayed and I offered them up to the Lord, I felt His peace and joy come over me, and now I know that as I continue to work and do what I have always done, it is my ministry to God, and I am a full-time minister of Jesus. What joy it will be to me as I work with Him and for Him."

During another conference in Astrakhan, Russia, I was on the stage teaching and preaching when all of a sudden a large, well-dressed Russian gentleman walked onto the stage shouting loudly in broken English, saying, "You come and stay with me; we do business together."

I had been staying in the pastor's house, sleeping on the floor in a typical, austere, utilitarian, communist-era apartment. I thought this could be a good deal more comfortable and very interesting. But as I looked a bit closer at him, I thought, "What if he is part of the mafia, a gangster? I could get murdered in my bed or kidnapped." I decided caution was the better part of valor, and I said, "Dear brother, let's talk about this later after the meeting," and I continued speaking to the congregation.

After I finished speaking, I made a beeline for the pastor to check out the businessman and see if it was safe for me to stay with him, and he was happy about it. He gave me the all-clear, telling me that the businessman was a good Christian, and his whole family was involved in work for the Lord. So I moved into his house and met his lovely family.

One morning at breakfast, I looked him straight in the eyes and told him what I thought the Lord was telling me to tell him. "The Lord loves you and is pleased with your business and all your work, and it is acceptable to Him as you minister to Him. The church has considered it to be secular, without God, and in the past you have been told you must choose between your business and the church and that you cannot have both." As I spoke, he broke down and started weeping, saying that he had become so isolated and felt that the only value the church put on him was his money.

By the time I left, he was a different man with a sense of vision and purpose to grow and prosper his business. He was able to enter in to a more intimate walk with the Lord, working with and for Him and experiencing Matthew 11:28-30:

> Come to Me, all you who labor and are heavy laden, and I will give you rest. Take My yoke upon you and learn from Me, for I am gentle and lowly in heart, and you will find rest for your souls. For My yoke is easy and My burden is light.

During a trip to Bulgaria, I was told by some parents that after my visit to them their children had started to work so much better at school, and they had steadily moved up in the performance ranking of their classes from low down to near the top.

The parents realized this was because the children had received fully the revelation that their scholastic work was their ministry to and for Jesus, fully acceptable to Him; in fact, it was their mission, their calling at that time. They had the freedom to see that whatever discipline they went into for a career would be a work for the Kingdom of God and that they were in the Kingdom of God as they did it for Him.

Their destiny for the Master could be to become a scientist, mathematician, nurse, business person, mother bringing up a family, pastor, or missionary. In fact, the whole kaleidoscope of possibilities is open to them, and they are all opportunities to embark on a lifelong adventure working with and for the Lord.

How exciting! I believe that you will get excited as you read on and that it will change your life forever. Hallelujah!

Chapter One

THE START OF A COMPANY

THE START OF A COMPANY

In 1983, I felt the Lord telling me to give up my job. I had learned over the years that what starts as a gentle thought—a gentle prompt from the Lord—could over a period of time become a constant firm conviction, giving direction and requiring action on my part. I had cried out to the Lord for many years, asking Him to use me, call me "full time" for Him.

At the time, I was an elder of my church, fully committed to it, and busy about the Lord's work, as well as holding down my job as the United Kingdom (UK) and Ireland sales manager for a company manufacturing diamond cutting and grinding tools for use in the stone industry. The job gave me the privilege of a nice company car and a travel expense account. It meant I could travel anywhere in the UK or Ireland, visiting potential customers and staying at some of the best hotels in the land, all expenses paid. I was also enjoying a rich family life with my wife,

Susan, and our four young children. We were secure financially, living in a lovely house, having all we needed.

I come from a working-class background. My father was a blacksmith, and my three brothers and I learned a trade as engineering apprentices in Devonport Naval Dockyard. I later became a research and development laboratory assistant at the Carborundum Company in Manchester, and it was during this time that I was born again at the age of 28.

After a few years, a job vacancy came up in the company for a production superintendent for the diamond products manufacturing department. I thought, "I should like that job—a big pay raise and a promotion—but I'm sure I wouldn't get it, and even if I did, I know I couldn't do it."

In my mind it was impossible, but I felt the Lord say, "If you want the job, apply for it."

I said, "Even if I got the job, I couldn't do it."

The Lord said, "If you get the job, I will help you do it."

Since we had moved from our home town of Torpoint in Cornwall, life had been very difficult financially. I was not afraid of work, and I usually had an evening part-time job serving customers in a local gas station to help the finances. The increase in salary this job offered would make all the difference to us as a family. It would mean I shouldn't need to work in the evenings, so I would have more time to spend with the family.

I decided to believe the Lord when He said He would help me, and I applied for the job. I prayed and tried to exercise what faith I had, and I was pleasantly surprised to get the job. I was learning that God was even interested in my work and that He knew about our financial situation and had a plan to get us out of debt.

Affecting the Workplace

When I started my new job, the trade unions were particularly militant in the UK, which meant that I as the superintendent was challenged on almost every decision I made to improve the performance of the department. If I did not address an employee in exactly the right way or if I said something slightly progressive, I could have a serious visit from the union shop steward, who was quite capable of calling the workers out on strike, causing chaos! I relied on the Lord and on the Kingdom of God within me, and over a period of time I was successful in building a team spirit and mutual trust, resulting in an efficient, well-performing department, meeting the production targets set for it.

I requested the removal of all the pornographic magazine pages that were a favorite with the men, who usually displayed them near their working place. They complied, I felt, more from a respect for me than because of my authority. I also noticed that the swearing and blaspheming virtually stopped in the department while I was around without my saying a word, simply because I set an example and let them know I was a Christian. I had the faith to believe that the Kingdom of God was in me and was flowing out of me like a river of living water, affecting and changing the very atmosphere and culture of the department. I was gaining the respect of my managers, the union shop stewards, and the workers of the company. Proverbs 3:3-4 was beginning to happen: "Let not mercy and truth forsake you…and so find favor and high esteem in the sight of God and man." I was finding favor in the sight of God and man!

The diamond production department had been placed in a secure part of the main factory and had no windows, which meant that during the shorter days of winter I came and went in the dark, barely seeing the light of day during the working week. I found this particularly hard, as I had been brought up in the beautiful Cornish countryside and as a boy spent as much time as possible outside, enjoying nature. I loved the sun, sky, clouds, trees, and God's entire kaleidoscope of shapes and colors.

I remember the very first morning after my conversion. The night before I had given my life to Christ, asking Him to become my Lord and Savior, and I had felt the Holy Spirit come into my life. I was born again. As I stepped outside on that beautiful May morning, I was so surprised because the green leaves on the trees, the blue sky, and the puffy white clouds seemed even more vivid and full of life than they had ever been before, refreshing my inner being. It was as if I had seen them on a black and white television until then, but now I was seeing them in full color.

At this time, I was reading the praise books written by Merlin Carruthers, *Prison to Praise* and *Power in Praise*. Inspired by what they taught, I decided to believe Scriptures like Romans 8:28, which says, "And we know that all things work together for good to those who love God, to those who are the called according to His purpose," and praise the Lord for my new, dark, five-day working week. I found this sacrifice of praise to Him drew me closer to the Holy Spirit; He was with me in a very real way, helping me to do my job.

It was exciting, fulfilling, and challenging, working with the Lord to make the department more successful at meeting the monthly production targets and keeping the expenditure for the department within budget. In fact, over a period of three years the department's production increased by 20 percent with little increase in costs. I was learning that God calls us to be winners like Him, definitely not losers.

About three years after my appointment as department supervisor, another opportunity occurred within the company—a vacancy for a sales engineer. It was a more senior post than the one I had, better paid, with a company car and expense account. It entailed traveling all over the UK and Ireland, calling on customers and selling them our range of products as well as some others we bought for resale.

Most of the stone customers at that time were situated outside the cities, near stone quarries in beautiful areas of the country. This meant that the sales engineer would be heading out of the city in the morning, while everybody else was traveling in to work. I thought how wonderful it would be spending the whole day traveling under the sky and sun, seeing the countryside, new sights and sounds, all at someone else's expense.

Again I said to the Lord, "I should love that job, but there's no way I could do it or get it."

The Lord said to me, "If you want that job, apply for it and I will help you do it." I had no sales experience and little self-confidence at that time; the thought of calling on complete strangers and engaging them in constructive conversation was a daunting prospect for me. I even choked on my food sometimes when I was eating in public if I thought people were looking at me. Such was my ill-placed timidity and fear of man.

Well, I thought, the Lord had helped me slay a lion by being a successful production superintendent. Perhaps with His help I could now slay a giant and become a successful sales engineer. When I told my boss I was going to apply for the job, he laughed and said, "You couldn't do that job, and what's more there is no way they would offer it to you. What do you know about selling?"

I applied for the job and went for the interviews, and they offered me the job. What a day when I collected my new company car! Until then I had owned some rather old cars, so to drive a new one was like a dream come true. My dad never had a new car; in fact, nobody in my family had. When I got home that night with the new car, Susan and the children were so excited we all piled in and went for a ride.

It was a great time of praise and thanks to the Lord as I could see clearly how He had led me to this point. I could spend hours as I drove just praising and praying in the Spirit. I could stop briefly by a river or stream and just tell Him I loved Him and feel His presence. I had a job to do but a freedom to organize it myself, and provided I got the sales, everybody was happy. No unions to concern myself with or other people's performance, just my own working with God.

I learned that if you work hard and diligently, wanting to serve your customers as well as your bosses, in fellowship with the Lord, success as God and man measure it will surely come. I was very successful doing the job and grew greatly as a person. It was as if I had entered into something I had been designed to do. Each job that I had done so far—from my first, serving a five-year apprenticeship in Devonport, to my present job as the chairman of our company—has unlocked gifts and character traits I did not realize I had. I discovered that work reveals, matures, and refines a person when they work in it with their Maker.

> *That you may walk worthy of the Lord, fully pleasing Him, being fruitful in every good work and increasing in the knowledge of God; strengthened with all might, according to His glorious power, for all patience and long-suffering with joy* (Colossians 1:10-11).

When I told my fellow elders and the church of our plans to do what we felt the Lord telling us—to give up my job and look to Him—they were unable to witness to it and made it clear that they could not support us if we went ahead. Looking back, I am sure it was the right response; it served to test the authenticity of the call.

Testing the Calling

On October 14, 1983, I left my job and started "full time" for the Lord. I thought the Lord had called me to be a missionary, evangelist, or pastor, all activities that I had been involved in to some degree over the years. During the next five to six months, I spent much time working for the church and in prayer and fasting. I cried out to God to open the great effectual door He had prepared for me and my family. I felt certain that since God had told me to give up my job, a door of great opportunity for "full time" ministry for Him would open, a door that would also provide for our material needs. I was prepared to move anywhere for Him, home or abroad.

After four months, our reserves of money were used up, we were behind in our house mortgage payments, overdrawn at the bank, and getting deeper in debt as the days went by. Not a nice feeling at all! In fact, we were regularly receiving gifts of money from people in the church who, bless them, did not agree with what we were doing but were willing just to love us and support us through it all.

It was about that time that I started to experience what must have been some kind of depression. I would wake up in the morning and feel full of despair, as though I had no future and no hope for the future. I could almost observe with my spirit, my mind, and emotions wanting to end it all by committing suicide. As soon as I awoke, I felt the compulsion to end it all. I knew it was completely illogical—I had a lovely wife and children, very good friends, and brothers and sisters in Christ. I had good health and always had an optimistic outlook on life. I would always describe a glass as half full, not half empty!

I discovered more of the power there is in memorizing and speaking out the living Word of God at this time. I decided that

I should do just that, as soon as I woke, before the enemy could attack me. I would hit him first by speaking out the Word of God. The Holy Spirit gave me a mental picture of myself waking up and hitting a surprised devil full in the face, sending him reeling back from my bedside as I spoke out a Bible verse.

By memorizing and speaking out the Word, I was filling any space in me that the devil could fill with negative thoughts. The Word hit him hard before he could act, and it turned my mind and emotions to the truth—the real truth—of my situation based on the Word of God. I also muttered and meditated on the same word during the day and absorbed it like a cow chewing the cud.

After a few weeks, the attacks stopped, apart from a few random shots from the enemy which I quickly spotted and dealt with, using the artillery of the Word of God. My favorite applicable verses at that time were in Romans:

> *There is therefore now no condemnation to those who are in Christ Jesus, who do not walk according to the flesh, but according to the Spirit. For the law of the Spirit of life in Christ Jesus has made me free from the law of sin and death. For what the law could not do in that it was weak through the flesh, God did by sending His own Son in the likeness of sinful flesh, on account of sin: He condemned sin in the flesh, that the righteous requirement of the law might be fulfilled in us who do not walk according to the flesh but according to the Spirit* (Romans 8:1-4).

It was after this episode that I felt the Lord telling me to get another job. At first I thought it was the enemy pretending to be the voice of the Holy Spirit, but the pattern was familiar, one that I had walked on since my conversion. I thought perhaps he meant a part-time job, one that would pay the bills but leave me time to serve Him in the church. For a couple of weeks, I tried to find a part-time job—postman, milkman, even a taxi driver—but all these doors seemed firmly closed.

The conviction from the Lord to get a job became really firm, and I was becoming excited and not a little intrigued, wondering what the Lord was doing. Thoughts of a part-time job faded; I sensed the Lord was leading me into something big, something completely new.

One character gift I have from the Father is that He has given me a pioneer spirit, so I started to "think outside the box" concerning getting a job. I was drawn to look through the stone industry's trade magazine, and I noticed a product advertisement for a company which was the stone industry's sole agent for tooling for diamonds manufactured in Israel.

God Moments in Business

I felt the Lord prompting me to contact them and ask if they were interested in my selling their products in the UK and Ireland on a 10 percent commission basis. The prompting of the Holy Spirit was spot-on; He was prospering the work of my hands. The owner of the company invited me to meet him in London to discuss my proposal. I traveled by train, as we had no car by then, and made my way to a very expensive hotel to meet him. He was very smartly dressed and spoke perfect Oxford English. I felt so small and insignificant when I compared myself to him. But I was sure I was working according to God's plan and I explained that I had experience selling diamond products and knew many stone-working companies in the UK and Ireland and that I was willing to sell his portfolio of products for a 10 percent commission on every sale once he had been paid by the customer. I also heard myself say something I had not planned to say—that I should also like £300 (about $575) per month from him to help toward my selling costs. I could feel the presence of the Holy Spirit—it was what I call a "God moment in business." He smiled and agreed, and we shook hands on it. He was a nice man and he believed in me, and as I left the hotel I was floating on air. We were in business!

With the £300, I bought an old Triumph 2000. The car was very old but looked good, was sound mechanically, and was well cared for. I knew the owner quite well; he was a mechanic and he loved the car. So on June 5, 1984, I started driving all over the country visiting potential customers. The first month I sold £700 ($1,082) worth of tooling, the next month £3,500 ($5,411).

I had explained to my nice bank manager what we were doing and that no money would be coming in for a couple of months until the customers had received and paid for the goods I had sold them. He seemed comfortable with that and encouraged me by saying, "I am sure you will be very successful."

During the third month, I approached an Aberdeen-based company which manufactured magnesite abrasives suitable for polishing granite to a mirror-like finish. I made a proposal of 12 percent commission on all I sold and £200 ($309) toward my selling expenses. They agreed. "Thank You, Lord!" I now had £500 ($773) a month coming in and two ranges of products to sell during each visit. Even so, I could see that at the rate of growth of our sales it would be a couple of years before we were going to pay off our debts.

Then we had another "God moment in business"—one that could change everything. In October, I was calling on a customer in Hull. He greeted me by saying, "Bryan, I have just bought a new machine. It's brilliant; you should try to get the sole agency for it for the UK. It's just what the stone industry needs." I was finding it hard to conceal my excitement as I looked at this machine. I knew a good machine when I saw one!

My apprenticeship in engineering in the Dockyard was a real help at a time like this.

The opportunity to get the agency for the machine was amazing; what timing! What would have happened if I had not called on that customer that day? The normal reaction to finding a good machine was to keep it a secret since it gave them an edge over their competitors. The last thing one would do is encourage someone to market it and sell it to them. What's more, this particular customer was secretive in this respect and very ambitious.

I contacted the manufacturer in France and told them that I was interested in becoming their sole agent for their range of machines for the UK and Ireland and that I was actively selling into that market. I learned later that a large, well-known, UK-based company had also approached them with the same proposal, and that its manager spoke fluent French.

Following their invitation to meet them, I arrived in Normandy in December. I was ushered into the chairman's office and I sat facing the chairman; to my right sat the interpreter who was also the export sales manager. My perception was that this was probably the most important business meeting I had ever had in my life.

Prior to my coming to France, I had prayed and fasted for this very moment so that when I met the relevant people I should find favor with them. It was rather like Queen Esther when the whole Jewish nation fasted for three days for that split second when she came before the king unannounced, praying that he would not reject her, resulting in her execution, but that he would show favor to her and lift his scepter, the symbol of his power and judgment, allowing her to draw near to him and spend time with him and enabling her to accomplish God's plan for His people.

I was asked various relevant questions, and as we talked it was the time for another "God moment." I was becoming aware in my spirit that the export sales manager liked me, and he was explaining in detail to the chairman my answers to their questions. He even answered some questions for me without my saying a word, especially those relating to the work I was doing for the church. The chairman said that they would give me their decision in the near future, but since I was in France I should use the opportunity to look at their full range of working machines.

I was escorted by the sales manager to some of the customers using their machines, which meant I had the opportunity to show him what I knew about manufacturing in the stone industry and about machine engineering. Then another amazing thing happened—he introduced me to another manufacturer who made a range of sawing machines that would complement his range of machines. It would mean that if I were successful in getting the agency, we should have a complete portfolio of machines and tooling for any and every customer I visited. Both of these companies were innovative, dynamic, and in my opinion market leaders, hungry for business and expansion.

In December 1984, both companies agreed to give us the sole agencies for a trial period of six months. The sales manager (who, I learned later, was a devout Roman Catholic) and the owner of the company that manufactured the sawing machines came to the UK. They traveled with me and visited potential customers that I had chosen. It was a full, busy, rewarding week, and it enabled us to establish a good working relationship.

The Lord's timing was perfect. He had wasted no time and knew that the UK and Irish markets were hungry and ready for those types of machines. Consequently, during 1985 we moved out of debt into abundance, and by working with Him we have been able to grow the company to what it is today.

Main Concepts

- The sacrifice of praise to Him draws us closer to the Holy Spirit, allowing Him to be with us and help us do our jobs.

- The Lord might say to us, "If you want that job, apply for it and I will help you do it."

- We may think that we must be a missionary, evangelist, or pastor to be called full time for the Lord, but He wants to use us right where we are—in our work.

- Memorize and speak out the Word—it fills any space that the devil could fill with negative thoughts and makes those spaces the Lord's.

- The Lord's timing was perfect. When we wait on His timing, we set ourselves up to experience "God moments in business."

Chapter Two

YOU, WORK, AND GOD

You, Work, and God

The experience of God working with me in my employment and subsequently in establishing and growing our company caused a realization to grow deep within me that God didn't view work the way I had thought. This revelation made me look at the Scriptures more closely whenever work was mentioned or implied and examine it from a different perspective. I also read what few books I could find at the time relevant to the subject of work and God. Over the years with the Holy Spirit's help, I have arrived at what I want to share now.

Before I start, I want to acknowledge all the brethren of the Church who have had an input into my life through their books, preaching and teaching, or through their friendship.

Why Work?

First, I should like to define that all-important word work. The best and simplest definition I have found is, "Work is any creative physical or mental effort." For example, to study is work, whether in a school or university. To change the baby's clothes or sweep the floor or go to the well to get the water—it's all work. To labor on the building site or on the farm; to serve in the charity shop or help with the soup kitchen; to serve the church as pastor or teacher; to be an office worker or company director; to operate as an entrepreneur or business owner—it's all work.

We also need to ask the question, "Why do we work?"

The most obvious answers go something like this: "So we can eat and live; for our own prosperity; so we can have a house, a car; so we can have nice vacations; to supply our tithe for the church; so we can give financial offerings to God; to give us a tent-making ministry like the apostle Paul; to give us power and influence in the world; to tell people about Jesus."

There are many more reasons people can give for working, depending on their circumstances and where they live in the world. *These are actually the fruits of our work (the results of our work), not the reason we work.*

If we work for things, there is a great danger that we will become materialistic. The people in the kingdom of this world work for things, and they find no satisfaction in them when and if they manage to get them. As the economies of the poorer countries in the world improve and become more prosperous, there is a real danger that the believers in these countries will move into materialism very similar to what already exists in the Church in the more prosperous nations. If the Body of Christ can understand and embrace the real reason we work, it will make us perfectly balanced to enjoy the fruit of work without becoming materialistic.

The real reason we work? *We work because God has made us to be like Him, and He is a worker.* He has made you a mini-creator like Himself, to be creative, and He has given you the ability to visualize, imagine, plan, design, and manufacture.

No other created being has this creator ability; it is unique to humankind, because only man was made in His image *to be like Him.* The animals do not possess it; the angels do not possess it; the devil does not possess it. Humankind will create for purely aesthetic reasons, just because it looks good and is pleasing to the eyes, just to be creative and to be like God, productive and fruitful.

When God created man at the beginning, He honored him by creating him in His very own image. Can you imagine how this shook Heaven, how the angels must have gathered around to see this great event?

God gave man authority and power to rule over His creation, including every living creature, and in order for man to do a good job of it He made man in His image, to have His values, eternal like Him. *We are made with something of God's creativity, intellect, and skills—with the same capacity that God has to feel a sense of achievement, well-being, and satisfaction over a job well done.* We can see this satisfaction clearly in Genesis: "Then God saw everything that He had made, and indeed it was very good..." (Gen. 1:31). And in the first part of Genesis 2 we are told that He rested and declared that resting day as a holy day. I cannot help but get the sense that He relaxed and enjoyed being in His new creation, seeing it, touching it, smelling it, and hearing it. I believe He has put that same capacity in us; it's part of the package that makes us *like Him, made in His image.*

However extraordinary it may seem, God is really a worker and He enjoys working.

We are actually meant to work, to bring to fruit that inbuilt potential, and to fulfill the very reason we were born—our destiny. Entering into and fulfilling our destiny will always involve us in work of some kind.

You know that feeling when you have just cleared the kitchen of a stack of dirty dishes by washing and drying them and putting them away in the cupboard? Satisfaction, fulfillment of turning chaos into clean, tidy order. Am I the only one to feel that way about dirty dishes? For you it may be something else.

Did you know that Jesus Christ was a businessman? He was trained as a carpenter by Joseph, His father. There came a time when Jesus became the breadwinner for His mother and His younger brothers and sisters and took over the running of the family carpentry business.

Let's imagine Him working in His workshop, sawing and planing wood. There is a knock on the door. Jesus says, "Come in!" In steps a woman, smartly dressed and smiling. Jesus smiles back, "Hello Margaret, how are you? What can I do for you?"

Margaret answers, "I am fine, thank You; can You make me a table please?"

Jesus replies, "Certainly, what size table would you like?"

"Oh, six feet long, three feet wide, and eighteen inches high, please." (Remember this was before metrication!)

Jesus might draw a little sketch and show it to Margaret. "Like this?"

"Yes, that's fine, thank You. How much will it cost?"

Jesus Christ, the Son of the living God, has to work out how much wood He will need, the cost of the wood, and the time it will take Him to make the table, allow for His labor, and add on His profit margin. "It will be three *denarii* Margaret; is that all right?"

"That is fine, Jesus. When will it be finished?" Jesus Christ, the Son of God, has to work out a realistic finishing time for the table, taking into account the orders He has still to finish before He can start Margaret's.

The mental exercise could go something like this: Let's see now, I have a set of stools to make for Judas and a cupboard for Noah and there's Andrew's job, but I am waiting for the delivery of the wood for Andrew's. "It will be three weeks, Margaret."

"Thank you, I will come back in three weeks' time. Goodbye."

Three weeks later, Margaret arrives at Jesus' workshop. "Hello Jesus! Is my table finished?"

"Yes, it's over there."

"Oh, it's lovely. I didn't realize You were going to make such lovely legs for it. Thank You very much. Here is the money."

Now let me ask you some questions.

Was Jesus Christ less the Son of God as a carpenter than when He started His public ministry? Was He less spiritual as a carpenter working for His living with His hands than when He started His public ministry? Did He suddenly become more spiritual and more the Son of God as soon as He started His public ministry?

When He was baptized by John the Baptist before the start of His public ministry, the Holy Spirit came down on Him in the form of a dove and a voice spoke from Heaven: "This is My beloved Son, in whom I am well pleased" (Matt. 3:17). Up to this point, Jesus had only been a young student and a carpenter, and *God was fully pleased with Him.* Please note, fully pleased means *fully pleased. He could not be more pleased with Him!*

I'll let you in on a secret. God the Father and the Holy Spirit joined Jesus in His workshop especially to design and make those legs for Margaret's table. *And They enjoyed working together making them.* We really have to get hold of this fact. It's woven into His very nature—an integral part of Him. *He is a Creator God. He just loves working, making, renewing.* What a compliment, what a priceless gift He has given to us, making us like Him.

God has been—and is—constantly working. He is a worker; "It is God who works in you both to will and to do for His good pleasure" (Phil. 2:13).

We see Him working in the Old Testament, for example, dealing with the walls of Jericho, parting the Red Sea, inflicting the plagues on Egypt, and on into the New Testament to the Book of Acts. We see Him working on the day of Pentecost, empowering His Church, and later setting Peter free from prison and many other amazing works that continue to the end of Acts and down through the centuries to this present day.

I am compelled to repeat—we are made in His image. When we work, we fulfill the Creator stamp which is on us; we are agreeing with our Maker, cooperating with Him. We have been designed to work, and we operate best when we do just that—work. If we were made a car, we should be made to travel. If we were made a kettle, we should be made to boil water. We were made in His image; therefore we were made to work.

Unto the Lord

Colossians says, "Whatever you do in word and deed, do all in the name of the Lord Jesus..." (Col. 3:17). "Whatever" means whatever, which must include our work, assuming it is a good work. God said in Genesis 1 that His work was good and He rested; similarly our work must be good. Clearly, if our work is selling drugs or robbing banks, for example, they are not good works. A good work is one that benefits humankind; consequently, since you are part of humankind, it can also benefit you.

> *Slaves, obey your earthly masters in everything; and do it, not only when their eye is on you and to curry their favor, but with sincerity of heart and reverence for the Lord. Whatever you do, work at it with all your heart, as working for the Lord, not for human masters, since you know that you will receive an inheritance from the Lord as a reward. It is the Lord Christ you are serving* (Colossians 3:22-24 NIV).

When the revelation of what this Scripture was saying first hit me it took my breath away. Please do not miss it.

Paul is talking to slaves who, during Roman times, were considered animals that could talk. They had no rights whatsoever—the lowest of the low. They received no pay, there was no limit on the hours they could be forced to work, and they were given the very worst jobs and were often beaten and treated very badly. Paul is saying to the slave, *as you do whatever you are doing* (it could be the dirtiest, the worst job possible), *do it as unto the Lord; do it for Him and you will receive a spiritual reward for doing it.* This means that as the slave is cleaning out the dirtiest, smelliest toilet and as he is doing it unto Jesus in his heart, he will receive a spiritual reward from the Lord. *A spiritual reward for a work with his hands! I thought work was secular, not spiritual!*

Imagine slave Bryan cleaning out the dirtiest toilet you have ever seen in darkest Africa—you know, just a hole in the ground. An angel is watching with a notebook and pen, and he is saying, "Slave Bryan is cleaning that toilet as unto the Lord," and he marks down in his notebook one spiritual reward for him.

We must realize that spirituality is not an activity like going to church on a Sunday, singing, praying, prophesying, preaching, or going to mid-week church meetings. *Spirituality is a state of the heart, it's a position in the Lord, it's the Kingdom of God in us, and it's being in the Kingdom of God on earth.* Because of that state, we are spiritual and we make whatever we do on earth spiritual as we do it to the Lord. Going to church, preaching, pastoring, prophesying, praying, and working at cleaning the toilet. Is the fruit of our spirituality not our spirituality?

We must not be satisfied with the fruit, but the tree that produces the fruit. To be able to clean a toilet for Jesus requires us to be holy. Holy—separated unto the Lord. Holy—separated from our fleshly pride, ambition, and self-pity.

Notice the last part of Colossians 3:24: "It is the Lord Christ you are serving." Who is the pastor, prophet, teacher, evangelist, apostle, deacon, or worship leader serving? The Lord, just like the slave as he cleans the toilet with his hands, as he does it unto the Lord. *This means the slave is ministering to the Lord. His work is his ministry for the Lord. He is a full-time minister of the Lord just like them. He is a full-time worker for the Lord.*

*Slaves, obey your earthly masters with respect and fear, and with sincerity of heart, just as you would obey Christ. Obey them not only to win their favor when their eye is on you, but as slaves of Christ, **doing the will of God** from* *your heart. Serve wholeheartedly, as if you were **serving the Lord**, not people, because you know that the Lord will reward each one for whatever good they do, whether they are slave or free* (Ephesians 6:5-8 NIV).

Paul is stating exactly the same thing to slaves from this passage in Ephesians—that as they work, doing it unto the Lord, *they do the will of God and it is the Lord whom they serve.* They are His slaves, and as they do their work unto Him they minister to Him, not men, and they will receive a spiritual reward for their work.

If the slave's work is his ministry for the Lord, then it must be true for us also that our work, when done unto God, is our ministry for Him and to Him. It also means that if the slave is in full-time ministry for God, so are we as we go about our daily lives doing our jobs unto Him.

Just think about the work that you do and how *you* would be totally revolutionized inside if you started doing it for Jesus. Just think about the work that you do and how the *way* that you do it would be totally revolutionized if you started doing it for Jesus. Just think about the work that you do and how the *people* you work with or mix with as you work would be impacted for the Kingdom of God if you started doing your work for Jesus. The fact is, we are all called to be full-time ministers of the Lord as we do our work unto Him. Can you say, "I am a full-time minister of the Lord"? Did you hear that amen from Heaven?

Now the Lord is the Spirit; and where the Spirit of the Lord is, there is liberty. [Yes, while cleaning the smelly toilet.] *But we all, with unveiled face, beholding as in a mirror the glory of the Lord, are being transformed into the same image from glory to glory...* (2 Corinthians 3:17-18).

Paul never had to explain the position of work in the spiritual life of the normal, free Christian, because every Jew understood that work was a spiritual activity and was worship unto God. Every Hebrew boy, no matter how rich the family he belonged to, received training in a craft working with his hands. That is how Paul could have a business as a tent-maker—as a boy he had been trained in tent-making.

Do you think he was less spiritual when he was working on making and repairing tents? He had no problem; no divide for him. His tent-making was as much a part of his spirituality—of his ministry—as was his preaching, writing, and praying. Abraham, Isaac, Jacob, Joseph, and David were all businessmen; in fact over 80 percent of the people in the Old Testament were working or in business to make a living, and they walked with God and did mighty things for and with Him.

The Forbes 440 list identifies the 400 top performing companies in the United States of America (USA), and since about 3 percent of the population of the USA is Jewish, you would expect about 3 Jewish-owned companies to be in the top 100 companies in the USA. In fact there are over 40, representing an incredible 40 percent! When some kind of explanation for this phenomenon was sought, it was concluded that the work ethos of the Jewish owners of the companies was rooted in the Jewish culture that considered work to be a form of worship to God, *the root of the Hebrew word for "work" being "worship."*

Can you imagine how easily God is able to bless them? They are tuned in to the music and heartbeat of Heaven. The blessings have just got to flow down. What do we do? We tend to see work as a curse from the devil, secular not spiritual, and to be avoided if possible.

When the Roman Emperor Constantine decided that Christianity was to be the religion of the whole Roman Empire, his design for the church was a hierarchical one based on the one used to run the Roman Empire. And since much of Rome's cultural values were based on the preceding dominant Greek culture, it was only natural that the church propagated by the Roman Empire would adopt the Greek value system that declared emphatically that any manual work was a secular activity, suitable for slaves only, and definitely not a spiritual one. If Constantine had decided to seek out and copy the pure church, founded some 400 years before by Jesus Christ's disciples and the Holy Spirit with its values based in Jewish culture, the true spiritual nature of work would have become part of it.

Instead, we still tend to have the culture that states that to be really used by God and to live by faith requires that I give up my job and become a missionary or a pastor or church worker. As I stated previously, that was my heart cry for many years: "Lord, when are You going to use me? When are You going to call me full time for You?"

The church in the UK, for example, has been a victim of this inherent culture which, over the years, it has passed on to the church in many countries throughout the world through its strong missionary work. *How clever of the enemy to render 99 percent of the people in the congregations of the churches in these countries impotent, living out their lives without vision or a sense of calling for the activity they spend most of the hours of their lives on—working!*

How clever of the enemy to render the Church in these countries ineffective and quite unaware of its call by the Lord to operate in and dominate the marketplace. And how clever to keep it oblivious to the fact that the means to accomplish the Great Commission in Mark 16:15-18 lies in the hands of the 99 percent of the people in their congregations who are not employed by them. How clever of the enemy to neutralize work and the power, influence, and wealth it can bring to the Church through the 99 percent of people in it who are not employed by it.

We have seen that the slave has a ministry to the Lord—his work—and that it is a full-time ministry, fully acceptable to God. In fact, it is God's call on his life, His designated ministry for him at the time. Even when it is simply physically cleaning the toilet or some other unsavory task.

God wants to work with us in our work. As we see the pastor, evangelist, or teacher working for the Lord in the church, rightly we fully expect the Holy Spirit to help them in their ministry with the gifts of the Spirit—speaking in tongues, words of knowledge, words of wisdom, gifts of faith, revelation, vision, and Holy Spirit power. It must be the same for the slave and for you and me. As we do our jobs and make business provide for the family as we do it unto the Lord, He joins us in our ministry for Him, to help us. So we can expect revelation, vision, wisdom, and knowledge to enable us to be very successful in our work.

Successful Partnership

Is God a successful God? Of course He is. He is a God who excels in everything; He has called you to excel in everything, including your work, and He is determined to help you excel. If I were to ask you how you could show me something of the glory of God, you might take me outside and show me the beauty of the sky, stars, moon, clouds, mountains, trees, or birds. It is interesting that you would show me God's glory by what He has made. It is the same for humankind. We see something of people's glory by what they have done and how well they have done it. It's a revelation of what is in them, in their hearts. We see something of a person's integrity, diligence, desires, and aspirations in his or her work and the way it is done.

For example, the famous pioneer engineer Isambard Kingdom Brunel designed and built the Royal Albert Bridge in 1859. It spans the river Tamar, linking the counties of Devon and Cornwall by the Great Western Railway system. It is quite near to where I live. It was a magnificent, innovative structure when it was built 150 years ago and remains so even today. It is one engineering feat of many left by him as a legacy. And even today, as people drive past it or travel over it, Isambard Kingdom Brunel is remembered with respect and awe.

We need to understand that God really does want to work with us; it will revolutionize the way we work and our success. In Exodus 35, we see an example of God working with man. In these verses, we read that the Lord gives His Spirit to Bezalel and Oholiab.

> *And He has filled him with the Spirit of God, with wisdom, with understanding, with knowledge and with all kinds of skills—to make artistic designs for work in gold, silver and bronze, to cut and set stones, to work in wood and to engage in all kinds of artistic crafts. And He has given both him and Oholiab son of Ahisamak, of the tribe of Dan, the ability to teach others* (Exodus 35:31-34 NIV).

This is the first time the Bible talks about the giving of the Holy Spirit to an individual in this way. Please note—it's not to a full-time church worker but to a manual worker. Not to call him out of his work to become a full-time worker for the church, *but to help him be successful in his work.* God and people working together. As the triune God—Father, Son, and Holy Spirit—work together, so we are designed to work with our God and others.

Look at Genesis and see God and slave working together as Joseph encounters one challenge after another.

Now Joseph had been taken down to Egypt. Potiphar, an Egyptian who was one of Pharaoh's officials, the captain of the guard, bought him from the Ishmaelites who had taken him there. The Lord was with Joseph so that he prospered, and he lived in the house of his Egyptian master. When his master saw that the Lord was with him and that the Lord gave him success in everything he did, Joseph found favor in his eyes and became his attendant. Potiphar put him in charge of his household, and he entrusted to his care everything he owned. From the time he put him in charge of his household and of all that he owned, the Lord blessed the household of the Egyptian because of Joseph. The blessing of the Lord was on everything Potiphar had, both in the house and in the field (Genesis 39:1-5 NIV).

What happens as slave Joseph starts to work? In verse 2 we read that the Lord was with him and prospered him. As he worked as though Potiphar were the Lord, doing all his hard work to the Lord, the Lord caused that work to prosper, to succeed. This meant he did a good job in a good time, and he may have discovered a better way to do it that enhanced the quality of the finish.

God *causes our work to prosper.* We can expect to be innovative, not stuck in the groove of how it has always been done. We can expect to be creative. New products, new services, new ways of doing things. In verse 3 we read, "When his master saw that the Lord was with him and that the Lord gave him success in everything that he did." God was working with man in his *employment*, causing him to be successful. Can you get hold of that? It is not secular to God; God gets involved. He will do the same for you in your employment. Potiphar confirms it for us as an eye witness and benefactor of Joseph's work. God blessed Joseph *and gave him success in everything that he did. Joseph had to work in order for his work to be blessed.*

In verse 4, we read that Potiphar was so impressed that he promoted him to the top job in his business, his household, and all that he owned. I am sure this did not happen in just a few weeks. Joseph had to work for quite a period to impress his shrewd owner enough to make him promote Joseph the slave to be his next-in-command. We must remember that we are in a marathon when it comes to Kingdom of God matters, but be sure that God wants you to be promoted, just like Joseph. He wants you to get that pay raise, start that business, or get a job.

You could be forgiven for thinking that Joseph had arrived, he couldn't get any higher—next in command to Potiphar, an officer of Pharaoh, the captain of the guard. But as we read on, we find in verse 39 that he ends up in prison, penniless, with the status of a criminal, not knowing how or if he will ever get out. We also see that his integrity is not breached in the slightest; he continues to be willing to work unto the Lord whenever he can.

How is it that in the whole prison Joseph seems to be the only one who shines so well at the jobs that he has been given by the jailer (which might be just scrubbing out his cell or something similar)? The jailer takes a risk and gives him additional work, which with God's help he does very well, so much so that eventually a position is reached where Joseph is promoted to manager and is almost running the jail. No wonder God can trust him to become next in command to the ruler of the most powerful nation in the world at that time! Who got Joseph that promotion? God. He caused Joseph to find favor with man by the use of a spiritual gift, while doing his *unpaid job*. He can do the same for you, even if you consider you are a prisoner or slave.

I wonder if Joseph promoted the jailer when he came to power. After all, he was a good judge of character and was willing to put the right man in the right job while running the jail. I think Potiphar's wife would be nervous though, don't you?

"To Him who is able to do immeasurably more than we can ask or imagine, according to His power that is at work in us" (Eph. 3:20 NIV). As we have fellowship with the Holy Spirit while we do our work, run our business, and set our targets and goals with the Holy Spirit's help, we are allowed to imagine them reached; imagine we are successful at getting the sales required; getting the job we were after; getting the pay raise or the promotion; starting or expanding our own business; doing the housework or planting the garden.

> *All a man's ways seem innocent to him, but motives are weighed by the lord. Commit to the Lord whatever you do, and your plans* [the things you imagine] *will succeed* (Proverbs 16:2-3 NIV UK).

This verse is saying that when our motives for work are right, we can commit our work—our plans, what we visualize or imagine—to God, and as we work at accomplishing them He will work with us and make them happen.

Planting a Vision

If you cannot imagine it, it will not happen. The point is that He cannot make it happen, nor can we by His mighty power at *work* in us, unless it is in us in seed form in our imagination (see Eph. 3:20). God showed Abram the millions of stars one night and said, "You will have as many descendants as these stars" (see Gen. 15:5). From that day on, Abram could hold that picture in his mind and imagine his many descendants. It was some twenty years later before he had his first child. The picture was the seed God gave him.

God gives us visions and dreams; He uses pictures to get us moving by using our sanctified imagination. Jesus used picture stories—parables—to impart concepts and values about the Kingdom of God and to fire the minds and imaginations of His followers to do Kingdom work. When He said that unless you become like little children you cannot inherit the Kingdom of God, He created a picture for us of a little, innocent child (see Mark 10:15). Since we have all been young children, it's a picture we can all imagine and enter into. Children love and understand and can communicate through pictures at a very early age. They don't need a keen, mature mind, just their open innocence.

They say a picture paints a thousand words. Let's learn to paint positive pictures of ourselves in agreement with what God says about us in His Word. I wonder what Joseph imagined as he worked as a slave? After all, he had had two vision-dreams from God; he may not have understood them, and he certainly was not encouraged by his father and brothers in them. But he definitely acted like a man with a destiny. That is exactly the way we should act and think and imagine. Why? Because if you are in Christ Jesus you have a destiny; God has a plan for you that encompasses your whole being, which is worked out as you minister to Him in your *work*, rest, and play. In Third John 2, the apostle prays for all believers when he says, "I pray that you may prosper in all things and be in health, just as your soul prospers." Your destiny is the full counsel of God's words—all the promises, all the wisdom, knowledge, and revelation—it's all destiny mandate stuff for you. God has no favorites, and I trust that I have now firmly established for you that it is God's will and part of your destiny that you succeed at your work; consequently, you can imagine yourself being successful as you do it unto Him.

For many years I have been engaged in the selling of stone-working machinery ranging in price from £20,000 to £150,000 (about $31,000 to $232,000). Many times I have imagined a brand-new machine taking off from the manufacturer's factory in France, flying through the air, and landing in the factory of a customer I was trying to sell it to, at the same time saying, "Thank You Lord for the order for [I would name the machine]. I set my hands to get that order. Please send out Your angels to perform Your word to me." The word I was *imagining* being fulfilled by the Lord was the promise that He would prosper the work of my hands and similar promises.

> *Bless the Lord, you His angels, who excel in strength, who do His word, heeding the voice of His word. Bless the Lord, all you His hosts, you ministers of His, who do His pleasure* (Psalm 103:20-21).

> *The Lord will command the blessing on you in your storehouses and in all to which you set your hand, and He will bless you in the land which the Lord your God is giving you* (Deuteronomy 28:8).

> *...Whatever he does shall prosper* (Psalm 1:3).

> *The blessing of the Lord makes one rich, and He adds no sorrow with it* (Proverbs 10:22).

> *That I may cause those who love Me to inherit wealth, that I may fill their treasuries* (Proverbs 8:21).

Spiritual Rewards

Over the years, these and similar promises from God's Word have become very important to me, enabling me to visualize and know that I am successful. Consider a world-class athlete—a high jumper for example. Before she is willing to attempt to jump over the bar, she imagines the jump in her mind and herself sailing over the bar. She has won the victory in her mind—in her imagination—before she jumps. God imagined the world; it was in His mind before He spoke it into being, and since we are made in His image we should use the same process. As we begin to believe the promises and use our holy imaginations, we give the Holy Spirit room and freedom to operate in us, through us, and around us, to accomplish all that we set our hands to do as we work. The Father's heart for you is that, like Him, you too will be successful.

Let's look at the spiritual rewards for working for the Lord. I believe there are many rewards, some stored up for us in Heaven and some that we receive during our time on earth.

> *For no one can lay any foundation other than the one already laid, which is Jesus Christ. If anyone builds on this foundation using gold, silver, costly stones, wood, hay or straw, their work will be shown for what it is, because the Day will bring it to light. It will be revealed with fire, and the fire will test the quality of each person's work. If what has been built survives, the builder will receive a reward. If it is burned up, the builder will suffer loss but yet will be saved—even though only as one escaping through the flames* (1 Corinthians 3:11-15 NIV).

Let's imagine a very well-known pastor entering Heaven. The heavenly hosts are cheering and applauding him as he receives his reward. Then there are gasps as they all look at another man who has just entered, because they can see the Lord preparing his reward, and it's massive even by heavenly standards! They talk among themselves: "Who is this man? He must have been a great evangelist or prophet."

"No," someone says, "he was a slave!" He had been a slave for 30 years, and for the last 20 years he had been ministering to the Lord and his master through his work. (Remember, no pay, long hours of work, and no encouragement as he does the worst jobs.) *Heaven sees and judges by the heart condition of a person.*

Remember the widow's mite recorded in Luke. Jesus could see into her heart, and He knew that she was willing to give her all for the Lord, a measure of how highly she valued Him and loved Him. She ministered to the Lord through her gift. Jesus said:

> *"I tell you the truth," Jesus said, "this poor widow has given more than all the rest of them. For they have given a tiny part of their surplus, but she, poor as she is, has given every-thing she has* [to the Kingdom of God]" (Luke 21:3-4 NLT).

Jesus was not criticizing the giving of the more well-to-do people, but He was saying that giving and contributing to the eternal Kingdom of God is primarily a heart condition thing.

In Matthew 20, Jesus told a parable about a land owner who hired some workers for his land in the morning, then went out and hired some more at lunch time, and still more later in the afternoon. When all the workers finished their work for the day, he paid them all the same. The workers who had been hired in the morning complained bitterly.

> *They said, "The ones who were hired last worked for only one hour. But you paid them the same that you did us. And we worked in the hot sun all day long!" The owner answered one of them, "Friend, I didn't cheat you. I paid you exactly what we agreed on. Take your money now and go! What business is it of yours if I want to pay them the same that I paid you? Don't I have the right to do what I want with my own money?"* (Matthew 20:12-15 CEV)

The quality of each man's work is measured by *the heart condition that only God can see*, not the number of hours he works. The Kingdom of God value system is completely different from the kingdom of this world's value system, which relies so much on position, attainment, power, popularity, wealth, and appearance.

I wonder if those workers who had been hired first allowed resentment to grow in them during the day as they watched the new workers arriving, cool and fresh, to start their work, while they were tired and hot. I also wonder if they acted or thought in a proud manner toward them, saying or thinking, "I was hired in the morning. Obviously the master considers me a better person than you."

God sees into the heart; we all need to be very careful as we serve the Lord. In fact, the workers who were hired later in the day did not know what they were going to be paid, because when they were hired the land owner said, "Come and work for me and I will pay you what is right [whatever I decide]" (see Matt. 20:4). They were willing to trust him for the amount they would be paid for their hard work.

A spiritual reward that we receive when doing our work unto the Lord, one that is eternal but can be received while on earth, is that we become more like Him. Work sanctifies us, with the result that our relationship with Him matures and we are able to receive many blessings from the Lord. "Blessed be the God and Father of our Lord Jesus Christ, who has blessed us with every spiritual blessing in the heavenly places in Christ" (Eph. 1:3). We start our Christian lives with a heart just like the one Jeremiah describes: "The heart is deceitful above all things, and desperately wicked..." (Jer. 17:9).

It is the Lord's plan that, as we learn to do our work for Him, our heart condition improves. "For it is God who works in you both to will and to work on behalf of His good pleasure. Do all things without murmuring and disputing" (Phil. 2:13-14 RAV). That is what the Bible describes as crucifying the flesh as we clean that smelly, dirty toilet, working long hours for no pay or encouragement. Let's read on: "that you may become blameless and harmless children of God without fault..." (Phil. 2:15). That is very strong stuff! The Lord is saying through the apostle

Paul to you and me that as we do our work for the Lord without complaining, we experience a character change. We become holy; we become like Him.

> *That you may walk worthy of the Lord, fully pleasing Him, being fruitful in every good work and increasing in the knowledge of God; strengthened with all might, according to His glorious power, for all patience and long-suffering with joy* (Colossians 1:10-11).

We see the same sentiment in these verses: "for all patience and longsuffering with joy." Paul is talking about character—a heart change. One of the biggest miracles God works in our lives is to change our inner man—our character—and it's a change I believe that we take with us into eternity.

As we read on, we see another two spiritual rewards revealed: "according to His mighty power that is at work in you." What happens when we "live a life worthy of the Lord, fully pleasing Him and being fruitful in every good work"? We are strengthened with all might according to His mighty power at work in us, to help us do it unto the Lord, to work with Him and work a character change in our lives that we may become more like Christ (and closer to Him) and to help us do our work exceedingly successfully.

The second spiritual reward is "increasing in the knowledge of God." As we work unto and with Him, we increase in our knowledge, understanding, and appreciation of Him. Because we are living in harmony with the Kingdom of God, we tap into its wisdom and knowledge and revelation.

Leadership

A friend from the USA, whom I met in Uganda while working there, sent me a secular book from the USA called *From*

Good to Great, written by Jim Collins. I can recommend this book to anyone who is or wants to be involved in business. Jim Collins and a professional team of researchers carried out a study in the USA that identified a number of companies that had made the transition from being good companies to being great companies when viewed by their performance on the stock market, their profitability, and their growth which had been sustained for fifteen years.

They wanted to discover why some companies become great companies and others don't. The study compared them with a group of good companies involved in a similar sector of business. What is very interesting for us is that the main reason found for their success was that each of them, unlike the good companies, had what Jim Collins calls "a level-5 leader." They attributed their sustainable success in each case to the level-5 leader and the team he created to work with him.

The characteristics they found in these level-5 leaders are not what one would expect for a secular company; one could be forgiven for thinking they would be ruthless, self-promoting, proud, greedy, unscrupulous, and have a desire for celebrity status. In fact, they found the opposite. They were humble team players, setting others up for success; they were modest, people who rolled up their sleeves and worked hard; they worked for the common good of the company first, then their own.

Being a Christian and being conformed to His image is not a disadvantage in the big, bad secular world of the marketplace; it is a big asset—it is the formula for greatness.

Main Concepts

- We work because God has made us to be like Him, and He is a worker.

- We are made with something of God's creativity, intellect, and skills—with the same capacity that God has to feel a sense of achievement, well-being, and satisfaction over a job well done.

- Spirituality is a state of the heart, it's a position in the Lord, it's the Kingdom of God in us, and it's being in the Kingdom of God on earth.

- As we work, doing it unto the Lord, we do the will of God and it is the Lord whom we serve, and He prospers the work of our hands.

- A spiritual reward that we receive when doing our work unto the Lord, one that is eternal but can be received while on earth, is that we become more like Him.

Chapter Three

YOU, WORK, THE CHURCH, AND THE MARKETPLACE

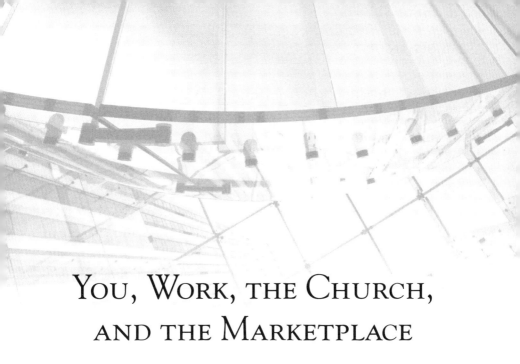

You, Work, the Church, and the Marketplace

I n this chapter, we consider the fact that our work has an important part to play in fulfilling God's redemptive plan for the world. In Matthew 5:13 Jesus said, "You are the salt of the earth," and in verse 14, "You are the light of the world." In Mark, He said, "Go into all the world and preach the gospel to every creature. He who believes and is baptized will be saved; but he who does not believe will be condemned" (Mark 16:15-16). The original Greek word used for "world" in these passages is *kosmos*, which means "society." Jesus was not just telling His disciples to move geographically but to ensure they were salt and light in the society where they lived.

Society can be defined as *social order, arrangement,* or *culture of a city, country,* or *area.* It is the social infrastructure that enables it to function in an orderly way. Sociologists tell us that society is built on seven pillars, and they are family, religion, business, education, government, the arts, and the mass media. Without these pillars, society would fall into anarchy, the law of the jungle would prevail. The fittest and strongest would survive, and the weakest and poorest would perish.

The last five pillars—*business, education, government, the arts, and the mass media*—are known as the marketplace of society. The marketplace is where the successful movers and shakers of society operate. They influence its value system, prosper, gain power, and steer society. If the Church wants to obey Christ's command to be salt and light in society, its members must be involved in the marketplace, succeeding and influencing society for good as they participate in it, fashion, influence, and have power in all of its five pillars.

We can see something of the impact the mass media has on the values adopted by society as they market the pop and celebrity cultures. The mere fact that most young and some not-so-young people judge their worth by comparing themselves with some celebrity is an indication of its ability to change our value system. And as each individual embraces a value propagated by the mass media, that value becomes endemic in society, with the consequence that the succeeding generation has little opportunity of rejecting it.

It is obvious that rich, successful business people have a profound effect on society, since they will do all that is in their considerable power to encourage a value system that is good for business. We also see modern politicians able to change the moral values of society in a remarkable way, so often steering legislation to follow the prevailing downward spiral of popular opinion, rather than fulfilling their mandate to be leaders, and leaders who will lead the masses into true values of morality, honesty, and service.

When one reads Titus 2, it becomes clear that even the lowly slave has a vital part to play in the church's marketplace ministry as he works for his master.

> *Teach slaves to be subject to their masters in everything, to try to please them, not to talk back to them* [or grumble], *and not to steal from them, but to show that they can be fully trusted, so that in every way they will make the teaching about God our Savior attractive* (Titus 2:9-10 NIV).

The master of the slave could be an ordinary family man or a very important Roman senator, businessman, or famous orator, but if the slave portrays something of the values of the Kingdom of God to him and his whole household, he is being salt and light in the marketplace. We are His salt and light as we reflect true Kingdom values while we engage in the five pillars of the marketplace. The slave doesn't need to say a word about the Kingdom (popularly called witnessing) unless invited to by his master.

The slave who practices Paul's teaching is the one who will be promoted to do the more responsible jobs, the tasks that may well give the slave some small privileges and possibly increase his sphere of influence—just like Joseph who, as a slave, worked so well that he was promoted by Potiphar to the position of Managing Director of his house and business.

The Church Today

We could say that the present worldwide Church falls into one of three camps. First is *the Church that compromises*. In order to remain popular, it compromises on doctrinal values and adopts or at least tolerates popular world values—for example, liberal sexual relationship values or liberal belief creeds not necessarily adhering to biblical principles. To be salt and light means that our Christian values season the whole cooking pot of society, but if we don't adhere to them, we as salt have lost our saltiness and will change nothing. Jesus said, "But if the salt loses its flavor, how shall it be seasoned? It is then good for nothing but to be thrown out and trampled underfoot by men" (Matt. 5:13). Christ never intended that we should compromise our faith in an attempt to be accepted by society, but that we should change society with our faith.

The second kind of church is *the fearful Church*. This sees modern society as a threat; its leaders want to protect their sheep from the influence society will have on them. They hide away, waiting for the Rapture. Not wanting to compromise their Christian values, they withdraw from any involvement in their local society. Basically, they are afraid of society and see it as a threat, something to be judged rather than to be saved. They quote Scriptures like, "Greater is He who is in you than he who is in the world" (see 1 John 4:4). But then they forget them when it comes to playing their part in influencing and changing society. It is very difficult if not impossible to change something if you are afraid of it.

"For God so loved the world [kosmos, society] that He gave His only begotten Son…" (John 3:16). God loves society. After all, when He made Adam He told him to rule over creation. This meant to bring order and establish godly values—in short, to establish a workable society with consistent godly values. When He gave the Law to Moses, it was to be the foundation and framework for society for His chosen people. The rule of society is a God thing first and then a humankind thing.

The secular world may think that they own modern society, but in fact it belongs to God and He wants it back; it should be part of the Kingdom of God on the earth. The second Adam,

Jesus Christ, has won back the dominion of it for the Church. He is just waiting for the Church to move in and occupy it. How? By its many members playing their part for God in the seven pillars of society with their creative, mental, or physical effort—their *work*.

God's call is for His Church to understand its mandate from the Lord and convert society—be willing to get involved in society—while maintaining Christian values and *holiness*, because as we saw earlier, holiness is not separation from the world, holiness is brokenness in our lives to the Lord. Holiness is living out the will of God as we do our work unto Him in the particular part of the *kosmos* where He has called us to minister.

The Church will not be manifest in the marketplace through prayer meetings or Sunday services, but by the church congregation rolling up its sleeves and engaging in the marketplace, education, business, government, the arts, and the mass media. By so doing they can influence and change it by bringing the Kingdom of God into their unique spheres of influence, their work within society, allowing the Holy Spirit to work in and through them, not in words of witness necessarily, but by being salt and light in it.

The main function of the church meeting should be for the healing, training, and equipping of the saints, to enable them to engage in society armed with the faith that their work is their ministry for God and with the gifts of the Holy Spirit, encouraged by the knowledge that their church elders and leaders are praying and fully support them as they do their Kingdom work—in the garage as a mechanic, in the café kitchen making lunches, or at home looking after the baby, for example.

I want you to meet "Betty." She is a young woman who works in a tax office along with 20 other people, calculating and word processing on a computer. Each Monday, she walks into the office with drooping shoulders and a miserable face as she contrasts her memories of the previous day's church meetings and her anticipation of a week in the office. All she wants is a week of Sundays, and it shows.

One weekend, Betty attends a Business in God conference where she learns that her work should actually be part of her worship and her ministry for the Lord. She is transformed as she takes this to heart; she goes to the office with a lighter step and a smile on her face. Her colleagues comment on her changed attitude, and her promotion is assured. She is able to witness to her coworkers in a way she could never have done before.

The Kingdom of God has come to the tax office—Kingdom values and Kingdom power helping Betty do her job with integrity and efficiency and to an excellent standard. She has become salt and light for Jesus in the office without preaching in the conventional sense of the word, and you can imagine it is only a matter of time before Betty is able to share her testimony with her colleagues, minister to their needs, and affect the culture in a profound way.

Engaging the Kosmos

Jeremiah 29:11 (NIV) says, "'For I know the plans I have for you,' declares the Lord, 'plans to prosper you and not to harm you, plans to give you hope and a future.'" A lot of us know and quote this promise, but when we look at it in context it is even more powerful and relevant for the worldwide Church at this time. Jeremiah is speaking to the remnant of God's chosen people who have just been defeated and taken into Babylon as captives. Babylonian society was in every way pagan and occult, a truly evil, idol-worshiping, decadent, immoral *kosmos*. How was God going to fulfill His promises, and what part were the Jews to play in it?

Jeremiah's prophecy was fulfilled some 70 years later when the Israelite captives were allowed to return to the Promised Land, but it also had a more immediate fulfillment which can be seen by reading the succeeding verses:

> *Build houses and dwell in them; plant gardens and eat their fruit. Take wives and beget sons and daughters; and take wives for your sons and give your daughters to husbands, so that they may bear sons and daughters—that you may be increased there, and not diminished. And seek the peace of the city where I have caused you to be carried away captive, and pray to the Lord for it; for in its peace you will have peace* (Jeremiah 29:5-7).

In the midst of a godless society, God said thrive and prosper, put down your roots, and establish businesses. Release and use the gifts and talents God has given you and exhibit the creativity of God. This is exactly what they did, and they did it exceedingly successfully. We can see this clearly with the rise to power of Daniel, Esther, Mordecai, Shadrach, Meshach, and Abednego—they all worked in society and prospered greatly, were promoted, and became great and powerful leaders, helping to shape the society they were in. These are only the few that we read about in the Bible; there were many others I am sure, less prominent, who succeeded in society and left their mark on it.

The Lord was indeed faithful to His promises made in Jeremiah 29:11; as they obeyed the Lord's instruction to engage in society, He prospered them and gave them a hope and a future. These promises echo down the centuries to us in this present hour. They are for you and me as we engage in our respective areas of influence in our particular societies by doing our work unto the Lord. We can believe and expect to prosper and walk in a hope and a future assured by Him who is worthy, our Lord Jesus Christ.

Israel was called and chosen by God to be His holy nation set apart, a kingdom of priests, His priests to represent Him to the unbelieving world. We see this when we read Exodus 19:6, "And you shall be to Me a kingdom of priests and a holy nation," and Isaiah 61:6, "and you will be called priests of the Lord, you will be named ministers of our God" (NIV). Before Israel could minister into the culture of Babylon, they had to engage in society and create relationships, and the same is true for us today.

We can see Jesus engaging with the *kosmos* in Luke 18:35. He healed a blind beggar; all the people rejoiced and praised God. In the next chapter, Jesus met Zacchaeus, a very rich businessman—a tax collector. He had heard about Jesus and was very hungry spiritually, so much so that he was willing to humiliate himself by climbing a tree to make sure he got a good view of Him. As Jesus neared the tree, He spotted Zacchaeus and immediately saw into his heart. In Luke 19:5, Jesus says, "Zacchaeus, make haste and come down, for today I must stay at your house." Zacchaeus' eager response was to come down from the tree and escort Jesus to his house.

During the ensuing meal, Zacchaeus is listening to and having fellowship with Jesus and is profoundly affected, despite the poisonous words of the nearby Pharisees, so much so that he declares, "Look, Lord, I give half of my goods to the poor; and if I have taken anything from anyone by false accusation, I restore fourfold"—a sure sign of repentance and that the Kingdom of God had come to Zacchaeus (Luke 19:8). This is confirmed in verse 9 when Jesus says, "Today salvation has come to this house." *Oikus* is the root of the original Greek word for "house" which Jesus uses in this passage. It means economy, which includes business. Jesus liberates Zacchaeus, and Zacchaeus liberates his business by bringing it under the rule of the Kingdom of God; therefore salvation has come to Zacchaeus and his business.

Jericho's society was impacted by this double conversion. The poor had some of their needs met; money was distributed into the economy. Society was affected because Zacchaeus was a very rich man. Jesus went on to say in the next verse, "For the Son of Man came to seek and to save that which was lost." Notice he said *that which* was lost, or **what** was lost. He was talking about a thing, not a person. I believe He was referring to the wealth and the power that goes with it, which up to that time had been lost to His Kingdom people. Part of His ministry on earth was to ensure that it was possible for His Church to receive back the wealth and power of the world. The first Adam lost it, but the second Adam, Jesus Christ, has returned it as part of His redemptive plan.

The Church is generally good at affecting the pillars of religion and family, but Jesus was also interested in changing all of society. That means the rich and famous, the bankers, corporate business people, entrepreneurs, and also *what they own and do*. We need to teach our children and young people to aspire to be rich, successful, famous business leaders, acquiring power and influence in our society, so that leaving school becomes a great adventure for them, where all things are possible as they plan and work with Jesus.

Faithfulness Training

In Luke 19, Jesus continues to teach, using a parable about money and trading in the marketplace with a story of a landowner who is going away for a long time. He calls his servants and entrusts each of them with the same amount of money. He gives each of them a mina and tells them to trade with it in the marketplace and make a profit for him, which he will receive when he returns in due time.

When he returns he calls them and asks each how they have fared:

> *Then came the first, saying, "Master, your mina has earned ten minas." And he said to him, "Well done, good servant; because you were faithful in a very little, have authority over ten cities." And the second came, saying, "Master, your mina has earned five minas." Likewise he said to him, "You also be over five cities." Then another came, saying, "Master, here is your mina, which I have kept put away in a handkerchief. For I feared you, because you are an austere man. You collect what you did not deposit, and reap what you did not sow." And he said to him, "Out of your own mouth I will judge you, you wicked servant. You knew that I was an austere man, collecting what I did not deposit and reaping what I did not sow. Why then did you not put my money in the bank, that at my coming I might have collected it with interest?" And he said to those who stood by, "Take the mina from him and give it to him who has ten minas." (But they said to him, "Master, he has ten minas!") For I say to you, that to everyone who has will be given; and from him who does not have, even what he has will be taken away from him* (Luke 19:16-26).

Was Jesus saying through this parable that the gifts He has given to His people for use in the marketplace, to help to fulfill His redemptive plan for society, should be taken very seriously and *not be despised and considered non-spiritual?* We all have gifts and talents—however basic we may consider them—whether they are manual, intellectual, or relational in nature. If used as unto the Lord, they will earn for us the same blessing as the servants with the ten and five minas—they both received a big promotion from their boss. They learned to use the little they were given wisely and with integrity. God wants us to use the talents and gifts He has given to us in the marketplace and succeed. The two servants we read about were wise and had developed their talents while the master was away, so that when they were promoted they had experience and their ability had grown sufficiently to take on the new task of running ten and five cities respectively.

This is also about our faithfulness with what He has given to us; He expects us to use them for His Kingdom in the *kosmos*. If we bury them or hide them away and don't use them, we are in danger of losing them and the blessing they could have brought to us (on earth and in Heaven) and humankind. On the other hand, the good servant who had earned ten minas was given even more. Why? Because the master knew he would use them profitably for him.

It used to be thought that to be used by God, one had to be called full time by the Lord as a pastor, missionary, or other full-time church worker or wait until one retired. In fact, 99 percent of church congregations are not employed by the church, but each one has a call to full-time ministry, working in society, being salt and light in it for the Lord.

Main Concepts

- We are His salt and light as we reflect true Kingdom values while we engage in the five pillars of the marketplace.

- God's call is for His Church to understand its mandate from the Lord and convert society—be willing to get involved in society—while maintaining Christian values and holiness.

- We need to teach our children and young people to aspire to be rich, successful, famous business leaders, acquiring power and influence in our society, so that leaving school becomes a great adventure for them, where all things are possible as they plan and work with Jesus.

- The gifts God has given to His people for use in the marketplace, to help to fulfill His redemptive plan for society, should be taken very seriously and not be despised and considered non-spiritual.

- Most people are not employed by the church, but each one has a call to full-time ministry, working in society, being salt and light in it for the Lord.

Chapter Four

WORK AND OUR COVENANT WITH GOD

Work and Our Covenant
With God

I want us to grasp and comprehend something of the heart of God toward us personally. If we look at the way God set up His creation, we get a glimpse of His intentions and desire toward humankind. We see as we read Genesis 1 a picture painted of a beautiful garden, the Garden of Eden; it was like a piece of Heaven on earth. Everything was provided for Adam and Eve— beautiful environment, gorgeous fruit, vegetables to eat, fresh, pure sparkling water, and friendship with all the animals; Adam and Eve at one with creation.

I remember an experience I had when on vacation in Australia. We were whale watching from a boat off the coast of Queensland when suddenly a huge sperm whale came alongside our boat and raised its head out of the water. I looked intently into his big eye as he came into view; he seemed to look back at me, and I fancied he almost winked at me and said hello.

It was as though we communicated and had an understanding of mutual well-being; it was a wonderful moment of communing with one of God's more spectacularly large creatures. If we multiply that experience by a factor of a million, we might get a sense of what it must have been like in the Garden for Adam and Eve, surrounded by God's wonderful creation.

They had very pleasant work tending the Garden, and every evening they had sweet fellowship with God as they discussed the work they had done that day and the things that had happened in the Garden. You can just imagine Adam and Eve telling God that Zimra the zebra had delivered her baby successfully that day, and what a lovely little baby zebra she was, so full of fun, running and jumping all over the place. Genesis 2:15-25 shows us that God had made Adam and Eve to be His friends. It didn't have to be that way, but that was how God desired it to be—that was His heart. And we know He is the same today as He was yesterday and will be the same tomorrow; His heart toward humankind—you and me—is still the same.

Fellowship

Lucifer, the fallen angel, came into the Garden and tempted Adam, and he broke fellowship with God by disobeying Him. Adam gave his God-given authority over creation to satan (see Gen. 3:17). Since that terrible moment, everyone born in the world has been born with a disease called *sin*, a deadly disease leading to death and separation from God. A curse came on Adam and creation—toil, weeds, and death (see Gen. 3:17-19).

God's fellowship with man was broken, but God's heart was still the same. He desired fellowship with humankind; He wanted to restore that working relationship with him. He searched through the land, looking into the hearts of the people, until He found a man called Abram, someone with whom He could have fellowship. God spoke to Abram several times in his life, and Abram always obeyed Him. In Genesis 12:1-2, God tells him to leave his homeland and go "to a land that I will show you." Later, God promised him many descendants and a special land (see Gen. 12:7).

A relationship is developing at the instigation of God. He is the prime mover, and He is the one who wants to bless Abram. God wants to bless Abram the man; that is still His desire, the same desire He had when He made Adam and put Him in the Garden of Eden.

In Genesis 14, we see Abram rescuing his nephew Lot and his entire household from the four kings—Amraphael, Arioch, Kedorlaomer, and Tidal. They had attacked and overcome five kings, among whom was the king of Sodom. Sodom was the city where Lot, Abram's nephew, lived; consequently, he and his household were taken into captivity by the four kings when they plundered Sodom. Abram not only rescued Lot and his household but also the king of Sodom's household and his possessions.

Now when Abram heard that his brother was taken captive, he armed his three hundred and eighteen trained servants who were born in his own house, and went in pursuit as far as Dan. He divided his forces against them by night, and he and his servants attacked them and pursued them as far as Hobah, which is north of Damascus. So he brought back all the goods, and also brought back his brother Lot and his goods, as well as the women and the people. And the king of Sodom went out to meet him at the Valley of Shaveh (that is, the King's Valley), after his return from the defeat of Chedorlaomer and the kings who were with him. Then Melchizedek king of Salem brought out bread and wine; he was the priest of God Most High.

And he blessed him and said: "Blessed be Abram of God Most High, Possessor of heaven and earth; and blessed be God Most High, who has delivered your enemies into your hand." And he [Abram] gave him a tithe of all. Now the king of Sodom said to Abram, "Give me the persons, and take the goods for yourself." But Abram said to the king of Sodom, "I have raised my hand to the Lord, God Most High, the Possessor of heaven and earth, that I will take nothing, from a thread to a sandal strap, and that I will not take anything that is yours, lest you should say, 'I have made Abram rich'" (Genesis 14:14-23).

Abram's response is very significant. In those times it was usual for the citizens to pay the king a tithe, or tenth, of their harvest or earnings as a sign that he was their chosen king. The king for his part had to ensure that the possessions and households of his citizens were protected, usually by having an army and by building a city wall. The king of Sodom was hoping that Abram, the successful warrior and businessman, would become one of his subjects, but Abram's reply is very firm, informing the king that the Lord God Most High was his King and Protector.

When we give our tithe to the Lord, we are declaring the same: "You, Lord, are my King and my Protector." The powers and principalities hate it; it stops them from being able to rob us and enables us to prosper and to glorify the Lord with what we have.

Covenant

In Genesis 15:1, we see God reassuring Abram after his declaration to the king of Sodom. He speaks to him in a vision and says, "Do not be afraid Abram. I am your shield, your exceedingly great reward." God is confirming that He is Abram's King and Protector. In Genesis 15, we read a dialogue between the Lord and Abram. God tells him that he will have as many descendants as the stars in the sky and that this land will be his possession. The relationship is maturing: "And he [Abram] believed in the Lord [knew Him], and He accounted it to him for righteousness" (Gen. 15:6). His relationship with God has become one based on Abram's faith in God. God could consider Abram as righteous before Him because of his faith, and therefore He could have an even deeper and more intimate relationship with him.

In Genesis 15:8, Abram says, "Lord God, how shall I know that I will inherit it?" He is saying, in effect, "Lord, I know You, but how can I be sure all these promises will come to pass? Please help me; You are a mighty God, I am a puny man; how can I be sure that what You say will happen?" What God said next must have blown his mind apart.

> So He said to him, "Bring Me a three-year old heifer, a three-year old female goat, a three-year old ram, a turtledove, and a young pigeon" (Genesis 15:9).

As soon as God said these words, Abram was in new territory. These were covenant animals used in the Middle East at this time, prepared in a certain way for the solemn ceremony to cut a covenant between two individuals, families, or tribes. We can imagine something of his thinking: "I know these are covenant animals, but whoever heard of God cutting a covenant with a man? Is God really thinking of limiting Himself to the terms of a covenant with me? What do I have to offer Him for my part of the covenant? He doesn't need anything from me!"

Let's look a little closer at the setting up and the terms of a covenant in Abram's day in the Middle East. Imagine there are two tribes—one tribe are hunter-gatherers, the other farmer-settlers.

The hunter-gatherers have a problem—the wild animals they hunt for food are becoming harder to find. The farmer-settlers also have a problem—raiders keep coming over the mountain and stealing their produce. The two tribes decide to make a mutually beneficial covenant, and their leaders come together to agree terms. The hunters agree to defend the farmers, and the farmers agree to provide the hunters with their produce. They would then negotiate the exact terms of the covenant, which could take up to three years to agree. They would be binding and irrevocable, with curses to fall on anyone who broke them.

The terms would go something like this:

- The tribes would each agree to share freely whatever they had with each other. They would probably have different working tools which could be useful to the others.

- They would defend each other, even at the risk of their lives, treating each other's enemies as their own.

- Each tribe's skills and talents would be available to the other.

Having agreed the terms, they would then perform a solemn covenant ceremony. The covenant animals would be cut down the middle and the two halves separated and lain opposite each other in a line. The leaders from the two tribes would then walk between the two halves of the animals. As they walked, they would say, "May the same happen to me as has happened to these covenant animals if I break this covenant." The covenant terms would then be recited by each of the leaders with the curses for breaking them. The leaders would exchange cloaks as a symbol of their respective authority and each would say, "My authority I give to you." They would exchange weapon belts and say, "Your enemies are my enemies. I will lay my life down for you if necessary." They would each give the other some valuable possession and say, "All that I own belongs to you."

They would then seal the covenant by mixing their blood from cuts on their wrists. The two tribes would then eat bread and drink wine and say, "This is my body; I will lay it down for you if necessary." The drinking of wine and eating of bread would be observed every time the tribes gathered together, to remind them of the covenant relationship that they had.

So, when God told Abram to prepare these covenant animals, can you imagine what Abram was thinking? "I have so little; is God going to be willing to make an irreversible covenant with me and commit Himself to fulfill the covenant promises? Is He who has everything going to say to me, 'Whatever I have is yours, and whatever you have is Mine?' Is He going to say, 'Your enemies are My enemies, and My enemies are yours? My power and authority are yours, and your power and authority are Mine?'"

In Genesis 15:10 we see Abram preparing and placing the animals as they would be for a covenant ceremony: "Then he brought all these to Him and cut them in two, down the middle, and placed each piece opposite the other." In the next verses, we see what God did:

> And it came to pass, when the sun went down and it was dark, that behold, there appeared a smoking oven and a burning torch that passed between those pieces. On the same day the Lord made a covenant with Abram [and his seed] (Genesis 15:17-18).

God could move the relationship on because of Abram's faith, and now God actually comes down to a level of relationship that the man Abram can fully understand, one that he can walk in and participate in. God actually confines Himself to it, He is obliged to fulfill it, and He is committed to it for Abram and his seed. It is important that we fully realize that our God is a covenant-making and a covenant-keeping God, covenant-bound to fulfill His promises to us, His covenant children.

In Galatians we read:

> ...*Though it is only a man's covenant, yet if it is confirmed, no one annuls or adds to it. Now to Abraham and his Seed were the promises made. He does not say, "And to seeds," as of many, but as of one, "And to your Seed," who is Christ* (Galatians 3:15-16).

The Abramic promises are yours; they were passed on to the Seed, Jesus Christ, and since you are in Christ Jesus all that He has is yours, and you also have the additional promises of the New Covenant.

Can you see Jesus saying, "This is My body, broken for you, and this is My blood, shed for you. Enter into a covenant relationship with Me, give Me all you have and I will give you all that I have"? You may think you have nothing to give Him, but you have what He treasures most, what He died for—*you!* This is very exciting if you are in covenant relationship with God through Jesus Christ, sealed by new birth through the Holy Spirit, born again.

> *Christ has redeemed us from the curse of the law, having become a curse for us...that the blessing of Abraham might come upon the Gentiles...* (Galatians 3:13-14).

The blessings and promises of the Abramic covenant are ours.

> *And if you are Christ's, then you are Abraham's seed, and heirs according to the promise* (Galatians 3:29).

> *Therefore know that only those who are of faith are sons of Abraham* (Galatians 3:7).

Hebrews 7:22 says that Christ is the Author of a better covenant with better promises. Our covenant is even better than Abram's! We have some new promises and all those of the Old Covenant, too. These are just a few of the new promises:

I will put My laws in their mind and write them on their hearts; and I will be their God, and they shall be My people (Hebrews 8:10).

And God raised us up with Christ and seated us with him in the heavenly realms in Christ Jesus (Ephesians 2:6 NIV).

Blessed be the God and Father of our Lord Jesus Christ, who has blessed us with every spiritual blessing in the heavenly places in Christ (Ephesians 1:3).

For as many as are led by the Spirit of God, these are sons of God. For you did not receive the spirit of bondage again to fear, but you received the Spirit of adoption by whom we cry out, "Abba, Father" (Romans 8:14-15).

Covenants at Work

When we consider our covenant relationship in the context of our work, it is very exciting because Abraham was a business-man and God made him very successful, rich, and powerful, so much so that he was respected and feared by the kings and tribal leaders around him. He truly made a big impact on the *kosmos*. This is true for all the patriarchs and heroes we read about in the Old Testament, such as Isaac, Jacob, Joseph, David, Solomon, Shadrach, Meshach, Abednego, Mordecai, Daniel, and Queen Esther. These are people God clearly caused to prosper, reaping the fruit of a covenant relationship with Him.

In Deuteronomy 8:18 (NIV) we read, "Remember the Lord your God, for it is He who gives you the ability to produce wealth, and so confirms His covenant with you." Wow! It is an integral part of the covenant that we should prosper and succeed in our work, in our business; God is committed to making it happen as a sign that He is in covenant relationship with us.

I first heard about my covenant relationship with God many years ago through the ministry of Kenneth Copeland, during the early days of the formation of our company. Some of those covenant promises became the foundation for its success. As I learned them and meditated on them, I felt I was walking on a rock, a certainty of success. All I had to do was keep working with my flesh and abide in His Word. These are some of the covenant promises that helped me so much in the early days, and now have become part of a solid foundation of faith for me:

If you fully obey the Lord your God and carefully follow all His commands I give you today, the Lord your God will set you high above all the nations on earth. All these blessings will come on you and accompany you if you obey the Lord your God: You will be blessed in the city and blessed in the country. The fruit of your womb will be blessed, and the crops of your land and the young of your livestock—the calves of your herds and the lambs of your flocks. Your basket and your kneading trough will be blessed. You will be blessed when you come in and blessed when you go out. The Lord will grant that the enemies who rise up against you will be defeated before you. They will come at you from one direction but flee from you in seven. The Lord will send a blessing on your barns and on everything you put your hand to. The Lord your God will bless you in the land He is giving you. The Lord will establish you as His holy people, as He promised you on oath, if you keep the commands of the Lord your God and walk in obedience to Him. Then all the peoples on earth will see that you are called by the name of the Lord, and they will fear you. The Lord will grant you abundant prosperity—in the fruit of your womb, the young of your livestock and the crops of your ground—in the land He swore to your ancestors to give you. The Lord will open the heavens, the storehouse of His bounty, to send rain on your land in season and to bless all the work of your hands. You will lend to many nations but will borrow from none. The Lord will make you the head, not the tail. If you pay attention to the commands of the Lord your God that I give you this day and carefully follow them, you will always be at the top, never at the bottom. Do not turn aside from any of the commands I give you today, to the right or to the left, following other gods and serving them (Deuteronomy 28:1-14 NIV).

Blessed is the man who walks not in the counsel of the un-godly, nor stands in the path of sinners, nor sits in the seat of the scornful; but his delight is in the law of the Lord, and in His law he meditates day and night. He shall be like a tree planted by the rivers of water, that brings forth its fruit in its season, whose leaf also shall not wither; and whatever he does shall prosper (Psalm 1:1-3).

The blessing of the Lord makes one rich, and He adds no sorrow with it (Proverbs 10:22).

Let's take another look at the story of the eagle and the chickens. I suggest you just read it again quickly to refresh your mind.

A young boy went for a walk up into the mountains of Scotland one day. As he scrambled over the rocks he came across an eagle's nest with eggs in it. He took one, put it safely into his pocket, and set off down the mountain to his home. When he got home he decided to put it into the nesting box of his mother's chicken pen. Sure enough, a brooding hen came along and looked at the egg, liked the look of it, and sat on it as though it were her own.

A few weeks later, the baby eagle emerged from the egg, saw all the chickens clucking away, scratching in the dirt, and assumed he was a chicken. He quickly joined in and copied everything the chickens did. They scratched in the dirt so he scratched in the dirt; they clucked so he clucked; they didn't fly so he didn't fly. They walked and ran around in circles a lot so he walked and ran around in circles a lot.

There were times, however, when he would look up at the big white-topped mountain in the distance and feel a deep longing inside. He would say to himself, "How wonderful it would be to be able to fly to the top of that mountain!" Then he would look at the dirt at his feet and at his fellow chickens and shrug his feathers and say, "But I am only a chicken." He grew bigger and bigger and was otherwise content with his chicken life, scratching around in the dirt, clucking as he walked and ran around in circles.

But there came a day (there always comes a day for each one of us) when he looked up and saw a mighty eagle soaring above the chicken pen. He had never seen one so close before; it was as though it was almost inviting the chickens to join him. "Wait a minute," he said, looking at the eagle and then looking down at himself, "I look more like that eagle than I do the chickens." He ran over to the water trough to get a glimpse of himself in the water. "I am sure I look more like an eagle than these chickens. I am going to try flapping my wings and see what happens."

So he started flapping, gently at first, feeling very embarrassed, because all the chickens were staring at him and starting to laugh, saying, "What are you doing, chicken? Trying to fly? Ha, ha, ha, how ridiculous!"

But as he flapped his wings he rose a good two feet off the ground. "Wow!" he said, "did you see that? I'll try again, much harder this time." And so he did, and before he knew it he was up in the air above the chicken pen. He shouted, "I am flying! I am an eagle, not a chicken! Wheeee! Whooo!"

As he rose higher and higher into the air he was amazed at how very small that chicken pen was; it used to be his whole world, but now it seemed so small and insignificant. He had such good eyesight that he could see for miles and miles all around him. He flew higher and higher, right up to the top of that mountain. The air was so sweet and pure up there, and it was so peaceful and quiet—no clucking, no running around in circles. He saw the beauty of the crystal clear rivers and streams as they cascaded down the mountain—all singing different songs but all in perfect harmony—and the many and varied little flowers of different shapes and colors. They seemed to carpet whole areas of the mountain slopes. It was so good being an eagle and not a chicken!

When we realize that we are in a covenant relationship with our God through Christ Jesus, we will start to see that we are no longer chickens but eagles. Our covenant partner is the King Supreme of the whole universe; He is omnipotent, omniscient, and omnipresent. He has made us children of the Kingdom of God; we used to be children of this fallen world who, like chickens, try to survive by scratching in the dirt, who are ruled by the curses we can read in Deuteronomy 28:15-68.

When the young eagle in the story started to fly, a different set of physical laws came into force to allow it to happen. The law of aerodynamics overcame the law of gravity that had previously governed its life and held it firmly to the dirt with the chickens. The enemy will tell us that we are still chickens. We tell ourselves that we are chickens, and the chickens we mix with will tell us we are chickens, that all we have are the curses. But there comes a day when we realize that we are eagles and we start to flap our wings and begin to soar on the covenant promises of God, promises that speak to us and empower us in every facet of our lives, including our work—our endeavors in the arena of the kosmos.

> *For the law of the Spirit of life in Christ Jesus has made me free from the law of sin* [with its curses] *and death* (Romans 8:2).

Main Concepts

- God had made Adam and Eve to be His friends, and His heart toward humankind—you and me—is still the same.

- When we give our tithe to the Lord, we are stating that all we have belongs to Him and that He is our king, our fortress, and our protector.

- A covenant is a mutually beneficial agreement between two parties that binds them together.

- The Abramic promises were passed on to the Seed, Jesus Christ; and since you are in Christ Jesus, all that He has is yours, and you also have the additional promises of the New Covenant.

- Abraham was a businessman and God made him very successful, rich, and powerful, so much so that he was respected and feared by the kings and tribal leaders around him.

Chapter Five

SPIRITUAL MOMENTUM

SPIRITUAL MOMENTUM

I hope that in the preceding chapters we have firmly established the fact that work is a spiritual activity, fully acceptable to God. In this chapter we are going to be exploring *spiritual momentum* and *discipline that leads to freedom*—the eagle-type freedom—what they are, and how important they are to us in enabling God to prosper the work of our hands and further the Kingdom of God on the earth. I have been able to put them into place and practice them in my busy life of starting and growing a company, being both a husband to my wife and father to our four children, as well as serving my church, usually in some kind of leadership role. I mention this not to score any points for myself, because it has all been and continues to be due to the grace of God on my life, but to underline that these concepts are meant for the ordinary, working Christian going about his normal Christian life in society.

We must consider discipline first, since without it we shall obtain little spiritual freedom or momentum. When a new army recruit arrives at the barracks to start his training, he comes full of anticipation, expecting to be taught how to fire guns, do hand-to-hand combat, drive tanks and armored vehicles, and generally learn how to fight for and defend his country. What happens? He is taught discipline; he learns how to obey. He is marched morning, noon, and night, and he has to do it in time with his fellow recruits in a precise and correct way. He is required to be smart in every detail, keep his boots cleaned so he can see his face in them; his bed must always be neat and made in the regulation way. Even his hair has to be cut to the army regulation length with little real style. Eventually he is taught how to fire guns, and he goes on training maneuvers.

After many months, there comes the day when he is sent out on live patrol in an area where there are real terrorists, real enemies. One day he is out on patrol with his ten-man platoon. Suddenly, from over the top of the hill close to them, a group of terrorists, with murder in their eyes and fully armed, comes running toward them. What does the new trooper do? Will he freeze with fear, be paralyzed by confusion? No, his training takes over; it bypasses his mind and his emotions; he acts instinctively as he has been trained. With his comrades, he moves swiftly into his fighting position and repels the attacking terrorists. He has been trained by constant practice until he will react correctly automatically; he knows he can do it because he has frequently done it in training.

God prepared King David—trained him by teaching him and helping him to slay the lion and the bear while looking after his father's sheep—so that when the day came for him to face Goliath, his training could take over and help him win the victory. Through discipline, our trooper has the *freedom* to be able to react in the correct way when attacked.

Consider the person learning to ski. At first it is very hard work, falling down in the snow. He seems to spend more time on his back than actually standing on his skis, but he disciplines himself not to give up but to persevere, painful as it might be both to his pride and his posterior. Slowly but surely he makes progress, and there comes a day (a day always comes) when his discipline has won him freedom, freedom to sail down the ski slopes, going wherever he wants.

The long-distance runner trains many hours, running each day eight miles, ten miles, or even more, day after day, week after week, month after month. While friends and family are enjoying themselves doing other things or just relaxing, the runner disciplines himself to run in the rain, the snow, or the blistering heat of the sun. Then comes the day when, after running 25 miles, he or she is the first over the winning line. All the people cheer, the media are there, photographers are clicking away. Some of the people looking on think, "How wonderful; I think I will become a runner—all that praise, the sense of achievement, and I'm sure they make plenty of money." But they don't see the investment of the discipline that has led them to the *freedom* to be able to run long distances fast, regularly, and when they want.

Spiritual Training

I realized early in my Christian walk that it was going to be more of a marathon than a sprint. I could also see, as we have explored in the preceding chapters, that I had all the resources I needed for success available to me in Christ. The keys to them are all there for me in the Bible, and I can have as much of God's provision for a successful life in Him as I want. God has no favorites, and I want to make sure I don't miss it. I wanted to be like the soldier, the skier, the long-distance runner, so I decided I was going to read God's Word from cover to cover systematically by reading three chapters of it each day, come rain, hail, or sun.

This is the foundation for our *first discipline*, which is to set aside a time each day to read the Bible. Quality time, prime time, the day built around the time, not time squeezed into the day somehow. Of course there may be days when circumstances will prevent it from happening, but as a general firm rule it must happen. We really are creatures of habit, usually bad ones that are of little profit to us. I guarantee that if you spend 30 minutes reading your Bible early every morning, after six weeks it will be much easier to do than when you started, and six months down the line it will be a valuable good habit you can build on.

The *second* good habit that should be accomplished at the same time you read is the keeping of a daily journal, which we will look at a bit later on. Reading the Bible from cover to cover? What about all those chapters in the Books of Numbers and Leviticus? They won't mean anything to me!

First, as a point of faith, because the Bible is the Word of God, we need to believe it's impossible to read it without it doing us some good. How does faith come? By hearing the Word of God. (See Romans 10:17.) If you don't hear it, how are you going to believe it? Believe all those wonderful promises we have been reading in the previous chapters, which are relevant to our daily living and our success in our work, in our businesses, and in all our endeavors. The Bible, God's Word, has more power than an atomic bomb. It has so much power for us all, and we have got to access it. You have got to access it.

Imagine having a tap and all the necessary plumbing in your home, but you keep going down the hill to the well with your buckets to collect water. Thirty minutes down and 45 minutes up, you arrive back at the house all hot and sweaty. All you have to do is go over to the tap and turn it on and get unlimited fresh, cool water! Imagine having electricity in your house with all the lights in place, but you don't flick the switch at night to switch them on; instead you light the candles like you have always done, and you see things dimly. When we read the Bible, we make it possible for the power to flow, for the revelation to come. It has statutes and precepts that can lead to your success, but you must read them to believe them and walk on and in them. Hosea 4:6 says, "My people are destroyed for lack of knowledge."

Second, if we don't read it, how are we ever going to be able to understand more about our God, the Father, Son, and Holy Spirit? As we read the Bible from cover to cover, we receive a growing revelation about His amazing, complex nature. He wants us to understand Him and know Him better in an informed way, and He will work with us and reveal Himself to us through the pages of the Bible, which is all about Him. This ongoing revelation of God provides a firm foundation for enjoying and being involved in the present wave of supernatural manifestations of the Kingdom of God on earth. Imagine you are going to meet the queen of the UK, but you don't bother to find out about her and how you should approach and honor her. Consequently, when you meet her you actually insult her without knowing it. She is very gracious and acts as though nothing has happened, nevertheless she is a little disappointed that you did not take the time and trouble to find out more about her; also your behavior does shorten your time with her considerably.

Third, as we read the Word, it becomes food for our spirit, whether we are aware of it or not. We make sure we feed our bodies several times a day if we possibly can, but we so often forget to feed our spirit. Reading the Word each day, whether we study and remember it or not, is not a problem to our spirit; to our spirit it is food, and even though our intellect seems to have received little from it, our spirit has received from it, as we commune with the Holy Spirit.

God's design for the triune man—body, soul, and spirit—is that the spirit, in fellowship with the Holy Spirit, should be in charge of decision making in consultation with the soul (mind and emotions) and the body. Our spiritual momentum will help to make this change occur. When we are born again, I believe we receive a finished work in our spirit man. "Blessed be the God and Father of our Lord Jesus Christ, who has blessed us with every spiritual blessing in the heavenly places in Christ" (Eph. 1:3). "If anyone is in Christ, he is a new creation; old things have passed away; behold, all things have become new" (2 Cor. 5:17). We need the sanctification of our soul; this is confirmed by many Scriptures in the Bible. When we catch glimpses of our pride, greed, jealousy, and desire to control, we have to say, "All things have *not* become new in my soul man." Such Scriptures could apply only to our spirit man. I believe our spirit man is full of the Kingdom of God, and as we learn to give him real freedom, which comes through our faith, and true humility in our soul man, it allows the Kingdom to flow out on earth, affecting our body and soul and all that we do. Jesus said, "He who believes in Me, as the Scripture has said, out of his heart will flow rivers of living water" (John 7:38).

Fourth, as we read the Bible, it allows the Holy Spirit to quicken a word or a passage to us which can be very relevant to our present situation and to what is going on in our lives at the time. These are called *rhema* words—living words for you from the Lord. They can be a lamp to your feet and a light to your path (see Ps. 119:105). The *rhema* word could be revelation of some aspect of the nature of God that your mind is able to hold on to, especially if you meditate on it. It could be a work of healing: "He sent His word and healed them" (Ps. 107:20). The rhema word can be so many things; it is a personal thing between you the reader and God the Author.

Fifth, the Word has a refining, sanctifying effect on us.

The Word of God is alive and active. Sharper than any double-edged sword, it penetrates even to dividing soul and spirit, joints and marrow; it judges the thoughts and attitudes of the heart (Hebrews 4:12 NIV).

The Word of God is truth, not to condemn us, but to liberate us and help to make us more like Jesus. Did you know God is dedicated to making you like Jesus? It is set in stone, and He will go to any lengths to accomplish this task. It's His number one priority for you. Why? Because He wants deeper fellowship with you; you are His friend and child and a brother to His Son Jesus.

Let's say you are going to start reading the Bible and journaling early tomorrow morning. Choose the most strategic time for you, but you will have to schedule it in, plan it, and stick to the plan to make it happen. All hell and your fleshly man will try to stop you. Start by reading the following chapters from the Bible: Genesis 1, Psalm 1, and Matthew 1. The next day read Genesis 2, Psalm 2, and Matthew 2. Mark all three chapters as a heading in the page for that day in your journal (homemade or bought). Over a period of time, reading each chapter consecutively, read through the Book of Psalms and on to the end of the Book of Song of Songs. When you have done that, repeat the process by starting the Book of Psalms again. From Genesis read to the Book of Psalms then jump over them to the Book of Isaiah and read to the end of the Old Testament, then back to the Book of Genesis to start the cycle again. Read through the New Testament a chapter at a time, starting with Matthew and finishing with Revelation, and then repeat the cycle by starting at Matthew chapter 1.

As you do this, you will receive *rhema* words from your daily reading from the Lord. Write them down in your journal on the day you receive them with any personal notes of how they apply to you and how you intend to walk in them for the rest of your life. You can also write to the Lord a little intimate love note of thanks for the personal living word He has spoken to you. You can revisit this event (it's eternal, suspended in space and time) by looking through your journal at any time. This will be a great help as you walk in the Word and the enemy tries to oppose your progress.

Renewing of the Mind

Our second discipline that leads to freedom is to memorize these words and speak them out every day. If you choose a small book for your journal, you will be able to carry it around with you. This will mean that you are meditating on God's Word every day.

> But his delight is in the law of the Lord, and in His law he meditates day and night. He shall be like a tree planted by the rivers of water, that brings forth its fruit in its season, whose leaf also shall not wither; and whatever he does shall prosper (Psalm 1:2-3).

Our brain is divided into two parts—the conscious mind and the subconscious mind. The conscious mind is approximately 15 percent of it, and it processes and analyzes all the information and various events that happen during our lives. It then files them away into the subconscious mind that comprises the remaining 85 percent of the brain. The subconscious mind stores them and forms concepts, beliefs, and conclusions from the information, which affect our thinking, our perceptions of things around us, and consequently our emotions. To a large degree, our belief systems are a result of our formed beliefs and concepts based on our experiences. When we become born again of the Spirit of God, a new dimension is added. Our spirits come alive to God; the Holy Spirit comes to live in us and starts to teach us the truth. Ephesians 4:23-24 says, "And be renewed in the spirit of your mind; and that you put on the new man which was created according to God, in true righteousness and holiness." Please note who it is that renews our minds; the Scripture says be renewed. We are the ones who work at it; the Holy Spirit and our spirit will surely help, but it is primarily our responsibility. How can this happen?

Imagine I am eight years old and walking along a road. A dog comes running up to me, barking and looking very threatening. The owner manages to get to it before it gets to me, but it has definitely frightened me. When I am 13 years old, playing in the park with a friend, suddenly a large dog comes bounding toward me and bites my bottom, not too deeply, but it hurts. By the time I am 30 years old, each time I am approached by a dog I feel afraid and just want to run away. I am a big, strong man and the dog may be quite small, but my subconscious mind has arrived at the belief that all dogs are dangerous, unpredictable, and to be feared. Even when I visit some friends in their home and their little dog runs toward me, I feel myself starting to tremble and sweat. The next day, however, my daily reading is Second Timothy 1:7, "For God has not given us [me] a spirit of fear, but of power and of love and of a sound mind." It becomes a rhema word for me; I write it down and I memorize it and mutter it every day. I feed it down into my subconscious mind to change that old belief and renew my mind. Faith arises from hearing it—in principle I don't need to be afraid of anything.

Three weeks later I visit my friends again. This time as I walk through the door I am saying to myself: "God has not given me a spirit of fear but of power, of love, and of self-discipline." That reminds me that I am much bigger than this little dog, much stronger, and probably much louder. I am free from fear, controlling my emotions with the Word, and I make sure I approach the dog looking and acting with confidence. He immediately picks up the message that I am not a man he is going to be able to intimidate, so he takes the submissive role. I win a victory that is only the first of a long line of battles that will last for the rest of my life as I combat the constant threat of various fears that will surely attack me during my adventurous life as a born-again Christian.

We know that negative words spoken over us or about us can be very debilitating and painful, but our real value can be seen in the truth of God's love letter to us—His Word. We need to read it and re-read it, memorize it and mutter it, and renew our minds; we need to flush out our subconscious memory, get rid of those old worldly beliefs, and fill it with the truth, God's Word, and His precepts and laws which are now ours since we have become children of the Kingdom of Heaven.

Spiritual Momentum

Those are the first two disciplines that lead to freedom. Now we need to look at *spiritual momentum*. To help us with this concept, imagine a very heavy bicycle, so heavy that as the rider starts pedaling, it moves very slowly at first. The rider is not over-exerting himself; he just needs to apply steady pressure for each downward movement of the pedals. As he keeps pedaling, his speed gradually increases to two miles an hour, then four miles an hour, and in a couple of hours he is traveling at a steady 14 miles an hour. He just keeps pedaling steadily, a motion that he can sustain for many hours.

Suddenly, as he is traveling along, he gets a fly in his eye. That hurts; he stops pedaling and tries to remove the fly. It takes him some time, but he remains traveling toward his destination. He has slowed down a little, but he starts pedaling again and continues his journey. After a while, he comes to a steep hill; he continues to pedal at the same rate as before and he sails up the hill without any extra effort. The bicycle just slows down a little, but he is able to continue his journey in spite of the hill and regains his speed on the other side of it.

What carried our cyclist forward when he stopped pedaling and helped to propel him up the hill? The momentum of the bicycle and the steady work of the cyclist meant that the heavy machine had kinetic energy stored within it. When difficulties and obstacles came along the way, the momentum, the weight and speed of the bicycle, kept it moving forward.

In the same way, we become unstoppable if we have spiritual momentum. The devil or the world may try to stop us, but our spiritual momentum will carry us through. The momentum comes from good spiritual habits such as reading, journaling, memorizing, and muttering the Word of God. As we practice them daily, they can be likened to the steady pressure that our cyclist applies to those pedals, a pressure that he can keep up for the rest of his journey. When things happen to us—the enemy attacks us, we may lose a loved one, or we may experience a similar tragic event—we can run on automatic mode. Our spiritual momentum keeps us moving in the Spirit, and by keeping to the good habits that are ingrained in us by constant practice, though our minds may be confused and our emotions all over the place because of what has happened, we are still able to continue our spiritual journey.

We can see from the example of the fear of dogs and from Second Timothy 1:7 that the Word has a spiritual momentum of its own, that as we memorize it and mutter it and practice and believe it, it will carry us through. The Lord showed me a picture once of a well in the desert; it was a beautiful sunny morning, clear blue sky, still, cool, early-morning air. He said, "My Word is like the water in the well. It is available for My loved ones, all they have to do is draw it each morning and drink it." The point is that we have to draw it. God has done it all so far, sending His Son and giving us the Holy Spirit, His Word, and His grace poured out on us in so many ways. But we are required to use our free will and draw and drink the water.

> *Hear, my child, and accept my words, that the years of your life may be many. ...My child, be attentive to my words; incline your ear to my sayings. Do not let them escape from your sight; keep them within your heart. For they are life to those who find them, and healing to all their flesh* (Proverbs 4:10,20-22 NRSV).

> *My son, do not forget my law, but let your heart keep my commands; for length of days and long life and peace they will add to you* (Proverbs 3:1-2).

> *Your word I have hidden in my heart, that I might not sin against You.... And I will walk at liberty, for I seek Your precepts.... The entrance of Your words gives light...* (Psalm 119:11,45,130).

I read and meditate on such words, and realize more and more that God's Word is life, and life more abundantly.

What an adventure to let down the bucket into the well of God's cool, refreshing, liberating Word every day and to drink it. Jesus said, "If anyone thirsts, let him come to Me and drink" (John 7:37). As we drink of the Word, Jesus through the Holy Spirit comes to us and communes with us. Our good habit, set up by pure self-discipline, driven by desire and hunger for God, and fueled by Jesus through the Holy Spirit, becomes a precious time spent with the Lord, a time of talking with Him, a time of receiving revelation and insight into and about His very nature, His character.

As we establish our spiritual momentum, it will have an effect on our position on earth; we start to gain access to what we need on earth and receive it from the Kingdom of Heaven. We draw it down according to what the Word says and with the authority of those who believe the Word. During my quiet times, I have often been aware that I am winning the victory for that day. Sometimes God would suggest that I contact a particular customer by putting the thought quite strongly into my mind. I have found very often that I have been in the right place at the right time to meet the right person to do good business or to find the right product to sell at the right time. "You will show me the path of life; in Your presence is fullness of joy; at Your right hand are pleasures forevermore" (Ps. 16:11).

Let's consider a desert that has had no rain for over five years. It looks very dusty and dead; you would think nothing good can come from it. But there comes a day (there always comes a day) when it starts to rain. Overnight, the desert is transformed into a beautiful garden, bright-colored flowers of all types blossom; it has become an exciting place, an exceedingly fruitful place, and all it needed was the rain. How could this happen? Hidden in the sandy soil there were seeds of all kinds, and since they had been there for over five years you could be forgiven for considering them dead and useless. But as soon as the rain soaked them, the life that was in them sprang up and started to bear fruit in a wonderful way.

It is the same for us—we have good seeds hidden in our lives, quite often in the areas we might consider deserts, and they can spring to life and bear fruit through the rain of God's Word to us. Since they are God's seeds that He planted, He knows all about them and their dynamic potential for you and His Kingdom. He has a plan to turn our wildernesses into fertile places, which will unfold as we cooperate with Him. "You crown the year with Your goodness, and Your paths drip with abundance. They drop on the pastures of the wilderness..." (Ps. 65:11-12). We can make this process possible and speed it up when we value God's

Word as He values it and apply it directly to what we do daily in our lives—our work.

I have already shared something of how I do this earlier, but basically we are allowed to command the orders to come in, as we start to telephone or visit customers, by using the Word that we have been muttering to ourselves. For example:

> *Lord, I set my hands to get this order for this (name the product you are selling) from my customer (name). You tell me in Your Word that You will prosper the work of my hands* (see Deut. 28:8), *so I command that order to come in, in the name of Jesus Christ. Lord, please send out angels to perform that Word and bring that order in when I visit him on Wednesday. According to your Word in Psalm 103:20, "Bless the Lord, you His angels, who excel in strength, who do His word, heeding the voice of His word." Help me to arrive at a strategy to get that order. Please prepare (name), that he will see what a very good machine we have, and that it is the best machine for the job. I clear the way for me to get the order, I clear any opposition from the enemy, and I bring that order, that provision, down from Your heavenly Kingdom where all my provision is. Thank you, Father; You have called me to be a success, the head not the tail; grant me success with this order and please add to it, show me what else he needs, and help me to see the other products that would really help him with his production.*

We can and must walk on the Word and make the Word work for us in our daily lives and work—whether we are a pastor, chimney sweep, plumber, housekeeper, nanny, slave, top company executive, entrepreneur, or business owner—and by so doing glorify God.

Main Concepts

- The investment of discipline leads to freedom and devil-crunching spiritual momentum.

- As we read the Bible and journal, we will receive words from the Lord that will renew our minds and align our lives with our Kingdom of God destiny.

- The Word of God is truth, not to condemn us, but to liberate us and make us more like Jesus.

- We need to read His Word, memorize it and mutter it, and renew our minds; we need to flush out our subconscious memory, get rid of those old worldly beliefs, and fill it with the truth—God's Word and His precepts and laws.

- Our spiritual momentum keeps us moving in the Spirit, and by keeping to the good habits that are ingrained in us by constant practice, we are still able to continue our spiritual journey.

Chapter Six

SPIRITUAL MOMENTUM AND THE PERSONAL GIFT OF SPEAKING IN TONGUES

Spiritual Momentum and the Personal Gift of Speaking in Tongues

Let's move on to our third discipline that leads to freedom, one that will bring an added dimension to our spiritual momentum—*the use of our own prayer and communing language, the speaking in tongues.* I am referring to the gift here in the context of private and personal use. I have found the practice of speaking in tongues every day while on my own both beneficial and possible for a busy working man with a business to run and a family of four children. As I drove around the country visiting customers, I spent many hours in the car. They could be hours when my mind was flitting aimlessly from one thing to another, creating a potential vacuum into which the enemy could feed anything, if I were not careful, so I decided to spend at least one hour a day speaking in tongues. I remembered an advertisement that ran in the UK encouraging people to remember to fasten their seat belts when they got into their cars, and I adapted it to help me set up a good habit. It goes like this: "*Clunk* (the noise of the door closing), *click* (the seat belt locking), tongues every trip." It may seem a little infantile, but I knew that in order for me to get into a good habit I should need a trigger to remind me, and then after a period it would become a habit. Now, every time I get into the car on my own, I automatically start speaking in tongues. I shared this in a conference in Africa recently, and a dear brother told me he started to do the same whenever he got on his bicycle; it was a signal to him to speak in tongues and it quickly became a good habit for him.

Tongues in the Early Church

Early in my Christian life I learned to value the gift of tongues, which I believe the Scriptures confirm is available for every born-again Christian. We read in Mark:

> *Go into all the world and preach the gospel to every crea-ture. He who believes and is baptized will be saved; but he who does not believe will be condemned. And these signs will follow those who believe: In My name they will cast out demons; they will speak with new tongues* (Mark 16:15-17).

Who will speak in new tongues? Whoever believes and is saved! On the day of Pentecost, we see 120 disciples baptized in the Holy Spirit with tongues of fire and a mighty rushing wind, and they all spoke in other tongues. In this instance, some if not all of them at this particular time were speaking languages of the many foreign visitors in Jerusalem. The amazing thing about the gift of tongues is that the language can vary depending on the oc-casion or circumstances and what the Holy Spirit is doing through and with us.

> *While Peter was still speaking these words, the Holy Spirit fell upon all those who heard the word* [Gentiles]. *And those of the circumcision* [Jews] *who believed were*

astonished, as many as came with Peter, because the gift of the Holy Spirit had been poured out on the Gentiles also. For they heard them speak with tongues and magnify God... (Acts 10:44-46).

Peter and the disciples knew the Gentiles had been baptized in the Holy Spirit by hearing them speaking in tongues. In Acts 19:6 we read, "When Paul laid hands on them, the Holy Spirit came upon them, and they spoke in tongues and prophesied."

First Corinthians 14 takes a closer look at speaking in tongues. Paul was writing to a church that had been allowing disorder and confusion to occur during their weekly public meetings by the over-use of personal tongues. There is a Holy Spirit tongue utterance that is given for the receiver to pass on to the church, which when interpreted becomes a prophetic word of encouragement for the church. It may have been that many members of the church in Corinth were speaking loudly at the same time in their own personal tongue. However, we can learn a lot about this precious gift from Paul.

For he who speaks in a tongue does not speak to men but to God, for no one understands him; however, in the spirit he speaks mysteries (1 Corinthians 14:2).

"Eye has not seen, nor ear heard, nor have entered into the heart of man the things which God has prepared for those who love Him." But God has revealed them to us through His Spirit. For the Spirit searches all things, yes, the deep things of God. For what man knows the things of a man except the spirit of the man which is in him? Even so no one knows the things of God except the Spirit of God. Now we have received, not the spirit of the world, but the Spirit who is from God, that we might know the things that have been freely given to us by God. These things we also speak, not in words which man's wisdom

teaches but which the Holy Spirit teaches, comparing
spiritual things with spiritual (1 Corinthians 2:9-13).

Edifying the Spirit

When we speak in tongues, we can be declaring the things that God has prepared for us that no eye can see or ear hear or mind conceive. We declare spiritual truths in a spiritual language; our minds may not know them, but we declare them, prophesying them over ourselves in a language taught us by the Holy Spirit. How cool is that! When the Holy Spirit showed me this, He reminded me about the seeds in the desert, each lying dormant, containing the fullness of the glorious plant that could spring up. I believe that the seeds planted by God in our deserts are affected positively when we speak in our personal spirit languages.

"He who speaks in a tongue edifies himself..." (1 Cor. 14:4). It is so important that we edify—that is, build up and encourage—our spirit to grow bold and strong. It is also important that we exercise him—help him to use his muscles and build them up. *Our battles have to be won in the spirit realm first, and then the victories are manifested on the earth.* How? *By our spirit leading the way;* after all, it is his domain. In Jude 20 (NIV) we read, "But you, dear friends, by building yourselves up in your most holy faith and praying in the Holy Spirit...." I believe Jude is talking about building up our faith by praying (speaking in tongues and praying in our mother tongue). When we speak in tongues, we build up our spirit man. Also our fellowship with the Lord through the Holy Spirit becomes sweeter and more intimate. Because the tongue that we speak comes from the Holy Spirit, we must believe (have faith) that He knows what He is doing and that what we are praying is going right to the target, doing the job, accomplishing the task.

But without faith it is impossible to please Him, for he who comes to God must believe that He is, and that He is a rewarder of those who diligently seek Him (Hebrews 11:6).

"For if I pray in a tongue, my spirit prays, but my mind is unfruitful" (1 Cor. 14:14 NIV). Imagine I am having a tough time in the office—two customers' big stone-working machines have broken down, and the customers are demanding quick action to get them working. One of my daughters seems to have a relationship problem at school that is occupying my mind, and I have just learned that one of our biggest customers is in financial trouble and owes the company a lot of money. My mind and emotions are in turmoil trying to solve the problems and understand what is going on. I am confused, I cannot think straight. I go out to my car, get in, *clunk, click*, I start driving and speaking in tongues. My mind is unhappy and fearful, but I keep praying in tongues, and after about 15 minutes, my mind starts to become "unfruitful"—quieter. The speaking of tongues has quieted it, calmed it, and made it unfruitful according to First Corinthians 14:14.

I keep praying in the spirit, and I start to see the problems from a Kingdom of God perspective, from my Kingdom of Heaven position. "...[He has] seated us with Him in the heavenly realms in Christ Jesus" (Eph. 2:6 NIV). I start to see the tempo and possibly the actual tongue language change; it seems to be more of a warfare, engaging type of tongue compared to the one I started with, which was my normal everyday tongue. I feel in my spirit I am making a difference; after a while I start to speak powerful, "bull's-eye" prayers in English. I continue in the spirit, praying in tongues and in English as led by the Lord. I return to the office some 45 minutes later, and I am able to deal with the problems as an eagle, not as a chicken scratching in the dirt and running around in circles.

"I thank God that I speak in tongues more than all of you. But in the church I would rather speak five intelligible words to instruct others..." (1 Cor. 14:18-19 NIV). Paul spoke in tongues more than all those in the Corinthian church, who seemed to use the gift a lot, so much so that they had to be cautioned about over-use during the service. I think we can say that we should not exceed the example of Paul's use of tongues if we speak for just one hour a day as a good habit, giving us spiritual momentum. After just a week of praying in the spirit for 20 minutes a day, one will feel and know that one's spirit is truly being edified and feel the benefits and be encouraged to aim for a minimum of one hour a day.

Main Concepts

- The amazing thing about the gift of tongues is that the language can vary depending on the occasion or circumstances and what the Holy Spirit is doing through and with us.

- When we speak in tongues, we can be declaring the things that God has prepared for us that no eye can see or ear hear or mind conceive. We declare spiritual truths in a spiritual language; our minds may not know them, but we declare them, prophesying them over ourselves in a language taught us by the Holy Spirit.

- The seeds planted by God in our deserts are affected positively when we speak in our personal spirit languages.

- When we speak in tongues, we build up our spirit man. Also our fellowship with the Lord through the Holy Spirit becomes sweeter and more intimate.

- Paul spoke in tongues more than all those in the Corinthian church, who seemed to use the gift a lot, so much so that they had to be cautioned about overuse during the service.

Chapter Seven

SPIRITUAL MOMENTUM AND PERSONAL FASTING

Spiritual Momentum
and Personal Fasting

Our fourth discipline that will lead to freedom is regular fasting. Creating and maintaining the good habit of fasting one day every week will add greatly to our spiritual momentum. Early in my Christian walk, I was inspired and challenged by teaching and preaching on the benefits of fasting; so much so that, though I was young in the faith, I thought I should experiment by abstaining from food and just drink water for one day every week for a month and see what happened.

Almost the next day after my first one-day fast, I was convinced it was the right thing to do if I wanted to grow in my relationship with the Lord and the things of the Kingdom of God. Since that day I have endeavored to fast one day a week, keeping to the same day of the week, to help establish a habit that my body, soul, and mind could follow and know that it was something that would happen, no matter how much they complained.

I am referring here to personal fasting, just you and the Lord. I am always impressed by the corporate fasting that is taking place in churches all over the world, but this one day a week is your personal fast as well as, or to blend in with, any corporate fasting and to be carried out during your normal working regime.

What does God's Word say about fasting and its many benefits? In Esther 3, we read of a plot to destroy the whole Jewish nation dispersed in the Babylonian empire. Haman, the instigator of a conspiracy against the Jews, exploited and abused his high position in the king's court to gain the king's stamp of authority on his diabolical plan which, once authorized by the king, was irrevocable. We read:

> And the letters were sent by couriers into all the king's provinces, to destroy, to kill, and to annihilate all the Jews, both young and old, little children and women, in one day, on the thirteenth day of the twelfth month, which is the month of Adar, and to plunder their possessions (Esther 3:13).

Stunned and shocked, confused and full of fear (Have you ever been there?), what do the Jews do? Do they run away and hide somewhere? No, they do a spiritual thing in the midst of a seemingly irresistible physical threat—they fast.

When we fast, we humble ourselves before God. "I humbled myself with fasting..." (Ps. 35:13). Every Monday when I start my fast, I pray, "Lord, I choose to humble myself before You today. It is the prime reason for my personal fast. I need to crucify my fleshly man, the one that is full of pride, arrogance, and all kinds of fleshly lusts." If I am willing to play my part in its crucifixion, He will play His part. He also promises to reward me if I am willing to humble myself before Him. For example, Jesus said, "Whoever exalts himself will be humbled, and he who humbles himself will be exalted" (Matt. 23:12). James says, "Humble yourselves in the sight of the Lord, and He will lift you up" (James 4:10). I believe part of that reward is the death of the flesh and the growth of the fruit of the Holy Spirit within me. Jesus said:

> *If anyone desires to come after Me, let him deny himself, and take up his cross daily, and follow Me. For whoever desires to save his life will lose it, but whoever loses his life for My sake will save it* (Luke 9:23-24).

Peter wrote, "God resists the proud, but gives grace to the humble" (1 Pet. 5:5). Humble yourselves, therefore, under God's mighty hand, that He may lift you up in due time. It will happen. Cast all your anxiety on Him because He cares for you. Be self-controlled and alert, because the devil prowls around like a roaring lion, looking for someone to devour. Humbling ourselves makes room for God and guarantees that He will lift us up in due time.

In Esther 4:3 the children of Israel fasted because they were *God's children*. It was part of their culture and discipline; it was almost an automatic reaction. *In the day of physical crisis do something spiritual—fast and pray.* Fasting can become a shield for us at times of crisis. The enemy had thrown so much at them that they could have frozen with fear and despair. Fasting would ensure that they did not give up, that they would be able to stand. Their minds and emotions would be in shock, confusion, and despair. By fasting they would subdue them and allow their spirits to commune with God.

Fasting drains unbelief away, brings unity in our hearts, subdues the dominant flesh, and liberates our spirits. If we trust in our flesh, that is unbelief; faith is trusting in God. The less we lean on the flesh, the more we lean on God. We see this operating in the account in Matthew 17 when the disciples were unable to deliver the demonized boy. Jesus explains why they were unable to do the job:

> *Because you have so little faith. Truly I tell you, if you have faith as small as a mustard seed, you can say to this mountain, "Move from here to there" and it will move...* (Matthew 17:20 NIV).

I believe that Jesus was primarily addressing the unbelief in the disciples that prevented them delivering the boy. Unbelief blocks faith. Mustard-seed faith is small but it is very pure, not mixed with unbelief.

Fasting enables us to see a way forward. Mordecai explains the plan to Esther by means of his servant—that she should go before the king and plead for her people (see Esther 4:7-8). Esther understandably does not like the plan:

> *All the king's servants and the people of the king's provinces know that any man or woman who goes into the inner court to the king, who has not been called, he has but one law: put all to death, except the one to whom the king holds out the golden scepter, that he may live. Yet I myself have not been called to go in to the king these thirty days* (Esther 4:11).

In verse 14, we can see that fasting has really done something for Mordecai's faith. He is sure that if Esther does not agree to go in to the king, the Lord will still deliver His people, but use another: "For if you remain completely silent at this time, relief and deliverance will arise for the Jews from another place..." (Esther 4:14).

Fasting can become a sword, sharp and to the point. Esther now uses fasting as a sword. We can jab the devil at any time if we just fast about a specific thing.

Go, gather all the Jews who are present in Shushan, and fast for me; neither eat nor drink for three days, night or day. My maids and I will fast likewise. And so I will go to the king, which is against the law; and if I perish, I perish! (Esther 4:16)

Esther asks the people to join her in a three-day fast and to pray about the specific, all-important moment when she would walk into the king's presence unbidden, unannounced—that she would find favor in his eyes and that she would be attractive and pleasing to him, so much so that he would raise the scepter and allow her to live, to draw near to him. All those people not eating and drinking for three days, for just one moment in time. When the hunger pangs struck and their mouths became so dry, they could not forget why they were depriving themselves; they became a prayer; they did not need necessarily to speak it out. The desire was in their hearts; their very beings were crying out to the Lord for that specific moment in time.

When we fast, we become a prayer; our hunger reminds us why we are fasting. When the recession of the early 1990's was starting to bite in the UK, business became very slow for the company and the future did not look too hopeful. I started a seven-day fast, as I continued to work, for an increase in orders for our products. I became that one-line prayer. If God didn't help us, we should be lost. Over the next six months— slowly at first, and in spite of the continuing recession—the orders did increase, and we came through the recession unscathed. Have you thought of fasting and praying that you will find favor with that company buyer you have been trying to sell your products to? Or for that business start-up, that job interview, or that exam?

At that specific moment for which all the people have been fasting, a pagan king has to go God's way, and he lifts the scepter and gives Queen Esther an audience; he even asks her what her desire is. She is so much in the spirit after three days of fasting—so in touch with the Lord—she follows His leading and does not plead her cause immediately, but merely invites the king and Haman, the enemy of the Jews, to a banquet to be held that day. In Esther 5:6, the king asks Esther again: "What is your petition? It shall be granted you." Esther, still obedient to the Holy Spirit, invites the king and Haman to another banquet to be held the following day, when she will make her petition known to the king.

> *Haman went out that day happy and in high spirits. But when he saw Mordecai at the king's gate and observed that he neither rose nor showed fear in his presence, he was filled with rage against Mordecai* (Esther 5:9 NIV).

His pride was now so puffed up, his reaction to Mordecai not honoring him was almost taking over.

> *Nevertheless, Haman restrained himself and went home. Calling together his friends and Zeresh, his wife, Haman boasted to them about his vast wealth, his many sons, and all the ways the king had honored him and how he had elevated him above the other nobles and officials. "And that's not all," Haman added. "I'm the only person Queen Esther invited to accompany the king to the banquet she gave. And she has invited me along with the king tomorrow. But all this gives me no satisfaction as long as I see that Jew Mordecai sitting at the king's gate"* (Esther 5:10-13 NIV).

> *Then his wife Zeresh and all his friends said to him, "Let a gallows be made, fifty cubits high, and in the morning suggest to the king that Mordecai be hanged on it; then go merrily with the king to the banquet." And the thing pleased Haman; so he had the gallows made* (Esther 5:14).

As we read on to Esther 6, we see Haman entering the king's court with the sole objective of speaking to the king about hanging Mordecai on his newly-built gallows that very morning. What he does not know is that God has been working. His people had played their part by humbling themselves before Him by fasting and prayer; now watch Him lift them up.

The king had not been able to sleep and he had decided to spend most of the night having the records of his reign read to him. In chapter 6 we read,

It was found recorded there that Mordecai had exposed Bigthana and Teresh, two of the king's officers who guarded the doorway, who had conspired to assassinate King Xerxes (Esther 6:2 NIV).

He asks, "What honor and recognition has Mordecai received for this?" and is told that nothing has been done for him (see Esther 6:3).

Because it is still early in the morning, he asks who is in the court and is told that Haman has just entered the outer court. He has him summoned, and with the need to honor Mordecai in his mind, he asks Haman a question: "What should be done for the man the king delights to honor?" (Esther 6:6 NIV). Haman is so puffed up with his own pride he cannot imagine that the king would want to delight in honoring anyone but himself; consequently he chooses options that would reward the recipient with the most prestige—wearing the king's robes, a unique honor.

Haman answers the king:

Then let the robe and horse be entrusted to one of the king's most noble princes. Let them robe the man the king delights to honor, and lead him on the horse through the city streets, proclaiming before him, "This is what is done for the man the king delights to honor!" (Esther 6:9 NIV)

The king then tells Haman to go and do what he has said to Mordecai. What a shock for Haman, who had come in that very morning with the intention of getting the man he was now obliged to honor hanged on the gallows! As you read on in the Book of Esther, you will see that this particular episode broke Haman's pride and flipped him to the other side of pride—fear and insecurity—which ensured his speedy downfall.

I encourage you to read chapter 9 and see the deliverance of the Jewish nation from their enemies. In chapter 10, we read about Mordecai's promotion:

> *And all his* [the king's] *acts of power and might, together with a full account of the greatness of Mordecai, whom the king had promoted, are they not written in the book of the annals of the kings of Media and Persia? Mordecai the Jew was second in rank to King Xerxes...* (Esther 10:2-3 NIV).

Jesus said the following about fasting:

> *When you fast, do not look somber as the hypocrites do, for they disfigure their faces to show others they are fasting. Truly I tell you, they have received their reward in full. But when you fast, put oil on your head and wash your face, so that it will not be obvious to others that you are fasting, but only to your Father, who is unseen; and your Father, who sees what is done in secret, will reward you* (Matthew 6:16-18 NIV).

Notice that Jesus says when, not if, you fast. This teaching was given during a discourse where he also taught about praying and giving, all activities that are meant to be carried out regularly. He also says, "Your Father, who sees what is done in secret, will reward you." Humble fasting is costly but very rewarding. God promises to reward us when we both humble ourselves and fast before Him. When Almighty God blesses us and rewards us, it is worth having; it's the absolute best for our lives and our loved ones.

Our fifth discipline to help us maintain our spiritual momentum is to take care of our physical body, which is the temple of the Holy Spirit, an earthen vessel containing all the treasures we have been looking at in this book and more. If that vessel fails prematurely, all could be lost. There are many promises in God's Word that we can walk on, relevant to and speaking specifically about our health and life-span, and as we engage in our disciplines that lead to freedom our bodies will certainly profit greatly from them. Having said that, I believe that we have to manage our bodies in the most beneficial way for them, in harmony with God's intentions for their well-being. God can really bless physical discipline, and if we are willing to establish the habit of taking some exercise every day, of making sure we drink enough good water, of eating the best foods to supply what our body needs, and of getting enough sleep, it will complete our spiritual momentum.

I encourage you to learn diligently all you can about the needs of your body. A good start would be the reading of a book written by Don Colbert, M.D. called *The Seven Pillars of Health*. For example, I have for many years endeavored to run about two miles a day along our local beach, at the same time muttering my memory verses (usually in my head). I also enjoy a brisk walk in the country, speaking in tongues to the rhythm of my steps, and if I have trouble going to sleep or wake up prematurely, I have developed the habit of running through my memory verses in my mind, with the result that I am edified, moving in the Spirit, and usually fall asleep. Sounds fun? It really is fun. It's called spiritual momentum and the enemy hates it!

> *You will seek Me and find Me, when you seek Me with all your heart* (Jeremiah 29:13 NIV).

Main Concepts

- When we fast, we humble ourselves before God. Humbling ourselves makes room for God and guarantees that He will lift us up in due time.

- Fasting drains unbelief away, brings unity in our hearts, subdues the dominant flesh, and liberates our spirits.

- Fasting enables us to see a way forward, and it can become a sword in our battle against the enemy.

- When we fast, we become a prayer; our hunger reminds us why we are fasting.

- Humble fasting is costly but very rewarding. God promises to reward us when we both humble ourselves and fast before Him.

Chapter Eight

YOU AND BUSINESS

YOU AND BUSINESS

So far we have seen that the activity of work fulfills why and how we were made and brings us to a place of harmony within ourselves and with our Maker. We have also seen that God wants to work with us and that our work is a ministry to and for Him, and it plays a part in the building of His Kingdom in us (sanctification and all its many benefits) and on the earth.

If you can agree with that opening paragraph and you are a Christian with spiritual momentum, I believe that you are ideally suited to climb the corporate ladder or to start and run your own successful business.

God has given each one of us a unique character and attributes, designed to help us to plan and succeed in our careers and businesses. Remember the servants who were given one mina. Each was given something to invest in the marketplace. Not one of them could say, "But you gave me nothing to trade with," and the same is true for us. It is important therefore, before embarking on a career or enterprise, that we understand ourselves as fully as we can so that we recognize and operate in the *mina* gifts God has given to each one of us.

Gifted

Romans 12:3-8 gives us insight into some of the character gifts given to us by God the Father, gifts that may well start at the one-mina level, but if invested correctly can grow to ten minas and beyond.

> *We have different gifts, according to the grace given to each of us. If your gift is prophesying, then prophesy in accordance with your faith; if it is serving, then serve; if it is teaching, then teach; if it is to encourage, then give encouragement; if it is giving, then give generously; if it is to lead, do it diligently; if it is to show mercy, do it cheerfully* (Romans 12:6-8 NIV).

There is a danger that the gifts of the Father may be considered to be only for use in the context of what is considered a "spiritual" activity—usually a congregational meeting of some kind—but since work is a spiritual activity, we must widen their relevance to our endeavors in the marketplace. Paul starts this chapter on the gifts of the Father by saying, "I urge you...to offer your bodies as a living sacrifice, holy and pleasing to God—this is your true and proper [or reasonable] worship" (Rom. 12:1 NIV). This underlines the fact that the gifts are for all the activities carried out by us while serving Him.

Let's look at the gifts a bit more closely:

- We can define the gift of prophecy as the God-given ability to speak persuasively.

- Serving: the God-given ability to serve or demonstrate love by meeting practical needs so that others can be freed.

- Teaching: the God-given ability to share the truths in such a way that people understand and learn them.

- Exhortation (encouragement): the God-given ability to advise and stimulate the faith of others to spiritual growth.

- Giving: the God-given ability to give generously.

- Leading or coordinating: the God-given ability to lead or influence others.

- Mercy (sympathy or empathy): the God-given ability to identify with and comfort those in distress.

The gifts of the Father are character gifts that we are born with in seed form. They are designed to grow, blossom, and be fruitful through the nurturing and encouragement of a good godly upbringing, by good godly parents, in a godly society. I suspect that most of us were not so fortunate as to be brought up in such an environment. However, all is not lost, because when we acknowledge Jesus Christ as our Savior and make Him our new "boss" (Lord), all our character gifts from the Father become sanctified, acceptable to Him through the atoning blood of Christ; the indwelling Holy Spirit, with His gifts residing in us, becomes our Tutor.

If we have the character gift of prophecy, for example—the ability to persuade people to go our way, the ability to communicate truths that people will want to act on—we can realize that perhaps we can sell things to people that we believe are good products that will serve the purchasers well. We may have a business idea or want to team up with someone we know who has a good business idea; we can be aware that we have the ability to sell the idea to potential investors.

The character gift of wanting to serve others will enable us to create a business that will serve others. As we do, it will be obvious to our customers that we sincerely want the best for them; our diligence to do this and listen to their needs will ensure that we can grow a good, profitable business.

Those with the character gift of being able to teach others—precept upon precept, line upon line, or by example—can be very useful in a high-technology business, as they have the capacity to convey the concepts. (A clue to identifying someone with this gift is that they are always hungry to learn new things, constantly seeking out new concepts; they get excited when they find new information and delight in sharing it with interested people.) They are not necessarily the best sales people, but vital for teaching all the relevant people in the organization.

The character gift of encouragement is so valuable for all those who excel in the other character gifts. They encourage their colleagues to move into and grow in their gifting, to the benefit of the business.

The character gift of leadership requires a diligence to avoid corruptive ways and a sense of responsibility to ensure that people are led into truth, not into deception. This particularly applies to business, where many a poor investor has been led by someone with this gift into a business idea that was not sound even from its concept, with the consequence that they lose everything. A good leader can coordinate and lead gifted people into the successful launch and growth of a company, but should always be willing to be accountable to the others in the project.

The character gift of mercy, meaning sympathy or empathy, and the character gift of generosity are needed to start a caring-type business—such as care of the elderly or the infirm with home visits to meet their needs—or some kind of training business to teach less fortunate people how to cope or to better themselves. These gifts enable one to see the needs in society and give a desire to meet those needs along with an understanding of how to meet them in a businesslike way.

Most of us have more than one of these character gifts, but usually one or two are predominant. Our desires, our passions, and our skills are usually a reflection of our character gifts. For example, if you can play the guitar well, it could indicate that you are passionate about music of some kind. The passion has led you to invest a lot of time in it, and you have received fulfillment and joy from doing it. You have learned to play, and you want to share your passion and the joy you get from making music with others. This may indicate that your major character gifts are encouragement and giving.

If you have a passion for and you are good at playing the guitar and you could earn a living by starting a business doing just that, you would be a very happy and fulfilled person. So, for example, you could start a business teaching the guitar and performing at public functions.

On the other hand, it could indicate that your main character gifts are prophecy and leadership, and you want to compose music to spread the message about feeding the poor or conserving the environment and similar important issues. Your main character gifts might be teaching and sympathy, so you want to use your expertise at music to create a better way of teaching people how to play and enjoy music.

I know these examples are simplistic, but I believe they give a useful glimpse of why we need to understand what God has put in us so that we can move in harmony with them and be better equipped when considering starting a business or going down a certain career path. The Holy Spirit is our Tutor, and as I mentioned earlier in this chapter, He brings with Him His gifts that can be active in our lives as we use our character gifting from the Father in the marketplace.

> *There are different kinds of gifts, but the same Spirit distributes them. There are different kinds of service, but the same Lord. There are different kinds of working, but in all of them and in everyone it is the same God at work. Now to each one the manifestation of the Spirit is given for the common good. To one there is given through the Spirit a message of wisdom, to another a message of knowledge by means of the same Spirit, to another faith by the same Spirit, to another gifts of healing by that one Spirit, to another miraculous powers, to another prophecy, to another distinguishing between spirits, to another speaking in different kinds of tongues, and to still another the interpretation of tongues. All these are the work of one and the same Spirit, and He distributes them to each one, just as He determines* (1 Corinthians 12:4-11 NIV).

I believe that each one of us can receive every one of the spiritual gifts outlined when the Holy Spirit wants to give them to us as the need arises. But He will have difficulty giving them to us if we are not in a place of faith to receive them in every situation in our lives, including our work.

Using the Gifts

Let's unpack the gifts a little. Verse 8, the message of wisdom: to receive a spontaneous applicable message, showing the best answer to accomplish God's will in a given situation. The message of knowledge: the ability to receive a spontaneous relevant message of previously unknown facts concerning a given situation.

Verse 9, the gift of (spontaneous) faith: the ability to trust God with unusual confidence, knowing that He will work out His aims in the situation. The gift of spontaneous healing: the ability to restore health miraculously to someone in the physical or emotional realms through a direct act of God.

Verse 10, miraculous powers (the working of miracles): the given ability to change the course of natural laws in such a way that divine intervention is the only explanation. Prophecy: the given ability to speak a spontaneous message of truth which God has brought to mind, one that is relevant for the time and occasion; it strengthens, encourages, and comforts others. Distinguishing between spirits (discerning of spirits): the Holy Spirit ability to determine whether a certain action has its source in God, man, or satan. Tongues: the gift of Holy Spirit-inspired utterance that enables a Christian to speak in a language unknown to the believer. Interpretation of tongues: the Holy Spirit ability to interpret words spoken in a tongue into the language of the listeners.

We could liken our character gifts from the Father to a boat with its sails up, ready to go. The gifts of the Spirit are the wind in the sails giving and regulating the forward movement and steering of the boat.

We may think that our own intellect, ingenuity, and creativity, coupled with our splendid character, will create the company or get us the job or promotion we desire. But we really are designed to be operating in the gifts of the Holy Spirit all the time. Just read the Book of Acts—it's all about the acts of the Holy Spirit through the gifts of the Spirit in and through God's people in Christ Jesus.

I am learning to discern and acknowledge that a lot of my previous and current good decisions are a result of the gifts of the Spirit working in me. For example, to be able to discern the spirit of a prospective customer, supplier, investor, employee, or employer is extremely useful in helping to make the correct decision or arriving at a business strategy.

The supernatural, spontaneous gift of faith is needed to launch the new product, open the doors of the new business for its first day of trading, attend that interview for the new job, or believe that when one gets to the customer in two hours' time one will be able to sort out the problem with his machine even if it means moving in the gift of miraculous powers.

The gift of words of wisdom, knowledge, or prophecy and the gift of healing ensure a fruitful meeting and conversation between my customer and myself, one that is profitable for the Kingdom of God (which is my business), my customer's business, his spiritual and physical well-being, and that of his whole family.

The valuable gift of speaking in tongues and the gift of interpretation of tongues have already been explored in the previous chapter. We must also consider the gifts of the Son to His church and their relevance to the marketplace:

> *And He Himself* [Jesus Christ] *gave some to be apostles, some prophets, some evangelists, and some pastors and teachers, for the equipping of the saints for the work of ministry, for the edifying of the body of Christ, till we all come to the unity of the faith and of the knowledge of the Son of God, to a perfect man, to the measure of the stature of the fullness of Christ* (Ephesians 4:11-13).

The apostle, prophet, evangelist, pastor, and teacher all have the Father's character gifts corresponding to their calling to serve the church.

For example, the person with the Father's character gift of prophecy has had his or her gifting developed by the Holy Spirit to the point where they are able to receive the gift of words of prophecy from the Holy Spirit for the church. Jesus has appointed them as prophet to His Body to be recognized by the apostles and the others in the five-fold ministry.

The apostle, however, would be proficient in all five gifts and able and commissioned by the Holy Spirit to move in them as and when he decides. If we consider the apostle Paul and his ministry for example, we can see that he moved in all five of them as he traveled and worked as a tent maker on his missionary journeys.

Even though Paul's call to serve the Church was personal and unmistakable on the road to Damascus (see Acts 9), he never actually gave up his business as a tent maker. What sort of an impact must the fact that he still worked with his hands to supplement his needs and help meet the needs of others have had on those he was preaching the Gospel to in the marketplace and those he taught in the church? No wonder he could say with great authority:

> *Anyone who has been stealing must steal no longer, but must work, doing something useful with their own hands, that they may have something to share with those in need* (Ephesians 4:28 NIV).

There are many other people mentioned in the Book of Acts and the epistles who were called by God to minister to the Church and who also worked or had a business—Lydia, Priscilla and Aquila, Barnabas, and Cornelius, for example.

I don't want to belabor the point, but we should be mistaken if we assumed that only those employed by the church can be part of the five-fold ministry to the Church. Christ is the one who appoints, and His Church is called to be in the marketplace. I believe it is time to recognize and encourage those who are employed in the marketplace, have an office, shop, or factory in it for example, who have been appointed by Christ to be market-place ministers, equipped with the gifts of the Spirit to minister and with a God-given authority to command and make changes to it as they participate in it.

I hope that I have shown that to be ambitious in a career or in wanting to climb a corporate ladder or even start a business is in tune with God's heart wherever we are at this present time, be it at school, college, university, without a job, or working. It is a high calling, and we must not assume that because of it we shall never be part of the five-fold ministry to the Church of Jesus Christ.

Starting an Engine

The following story is basically true, but I have taken the liberty of enlarging it somewhat to illustrate some basic business concepts. I remember many years ago having a big pile of sand delivered to my house because a friend was going to lay some paving slabs for me. The best the truck driver could do was to drop the sand in a pile in my front garden, which was some distance from our back garden where the sand was needed. I looked at what seemed a mountain of sand, and then at what seemed a very small wheelbarrow, and at the distance the pile had to be moved. All sorts of negative thoughts went through my mind— this will take forever, I shall be exhausted, I have more important things to do than move all this sand, etc.

I knew that no one else was going to move it, certainly not my wife or my young children, so I applied logic to the problem. If I make enough trips, it is inevitable that the pile will be moved from A to B; all I have to do is to keep going. I'll just concentrate on the journey I am on, not think ahead and feel despair that in spite of my last trip to the pile it didn't look as if it had gone down at all.

My vision was to see the pile moved from one place to another, and that vision became very important to me that afternoon. I asked the Lord to help me, and I praised Him that I had this task to perform. I set out feeling a little awkward; I was not used to shoveling sand and wheeling a barrow. We didn't even own one; I'd had to borrow this one to do the job.

I filled the wheelbarrow for the first time. It wobbled a bit and seemed to have a life of its own, but by the fifth trip I felt much more in control, and by the 10th trip I had discovered a slightly better way to position the wheelbarrow by the pile of sand. On the 15th trip, I tried a slightly different position once again and found this made it even easier; on the 21st trip I experimented by holding the spade in a slightly different way and found I could move the sand with a little less effort on my part. On the 26th trip, I experimented with the best place to put my spade into the pile to load the wheelbarrow. On the 36th trip, I became even more efficient by reversing the wheelbarrow up to the pile while it was empty, thus avoiding the necessity of having to turn it when it was full.

That day I built an "engine" to accomplish a task. I was an important part of that engine, and with the Father's character gifting and the gifts of the Holy Spirit the engine was modified until the task was being done in the most effective and efficient way I could do it with the tools at my disposal.

Let's suppose that I notice that one of my neighbors has had a similar pile of sand delivered to his house and it is lying on his front drive. I approach my neighbor with a business proposition: I will move his sand to his back garden for a fee. He agrees and shows me where he wants it placed, and the next day I do the job and earn my fee. I make sure I do a good job, a job unto Jesus; I clean up very well after the job, leave the paths and drive spotless, smarter than when I arrived to do the work.

Three days later, I receive a phone call from a man living at the other end of my street. He has heard from his friend that I moved a pile of sand for him and that I did a good job. He tells me that he has had some work done in his garden and he has a pile of earth that needs moving into a dumpster, and he asks me if I am interested in giving him a price for moving it into the skip for him. I visit him and give him a price based on the time I think it will take, calculated on the basis of my experience of moving the two piles of sand.

My sand-moving engine has become a business engine, able to generate an income, an embryo business, which is steadily gaining momentum, having two satisfied customers who would be recommending me to others with similar needs; in fact my second customer is part of the management of the local golf club, a man of some influence with many prosperous friends. Having set up my "engine," I could even employ someone else to do the work, teach them all I have learned, and let them get on with it, confident that it would be done in the most cost-effective way.

When we start a business, we create an engine—the business concept, the entrepreneurial idea, the vision—that will be the vehicle to deliver the service or commodity to the customer in the most pleasing and acceptable way for them while generating a suitable profit. Our preliminary calculations, observations, inspirations, and revelations tell us that there is a suitable market for what we are going to be offering. Thorough research has shown that the price people will pay for it is at a suitable level to generate a healthy profit when the costs of providing the service or manufacturing or purchasing the products have been thoroughly checked and double-checked, allowing for the incidental costs that might be incurred.

It is absolutely crucial that the research and detail are diligently examined, an engine design arrived at, and a practice run of the engine carried out. We need to share our ideas for the project with a trustworthy mentor or someone we are accountable to in our Christian circle. We should be prepared to share it with our trusted friends and let them have an input; we must not be so stubborn that we will not consider other people's views. We can consider and reject if necessary, but quite often there are precious grains of truth in what has been said that can be useful, now or in the future.

Once we start our engine, we must expect and be eager to modify it as and when we see the advantage of doing so. My engine for moving the sand had a momentum, and as it ran it improved. When we start our business engine, it gains a momentum that will carry us and our employees to success; the more we are willing to perfect it, the greater will be the success.

I said that I could have employed someone to run my engine for moving the sand, but it would have had to be the right person—someone with the right character who would catch the vision to move the sand in the most efficient and effective way. If we plan to employ someone to be part of the business engine, it is vital that we employ the right person, not just someone who is working for money, but someone who wants to be part of a success story, who understands and passionately embraces the vision and business ethos. It is better not to employ than employ the wrong person.

Be encouraged dear brother and sister; remember these verses are for you.

"For I know the plans that I have for you," declares the Lord, "plans to prosper you and not to harm you, plans to give you hope and a future" (Jeremiah 29:11 NIV).

Blessed is the man who walks not in the counsel of the ungodly, nor stands in the path of sinners, nor sits in the seat of the scornful; but his delight is in the law of the Lord, and in His law he meditates day and night. He shall be like a tree planted by the rivers of water, that brings forth its fruit in its season, whose leaf also shall not wither; and whatever he does shall prosper (Psalm 1:1-3).

Main Concepts

- God has given each one of us a unique character and attributes, designed to help us to plan and succeed in our careers and businesses.

- Since work is a spiritual activity, we must widen the relevance of the gifts of the Spirit to our endeavors in the marketplace and all the activities carried out by us while serving Him.

- Our desires, our passions, and our skills are usually a reflection of our character gifts.

- Each one of us can receive every one of the spiritual gifts outlined when the Holy Spirit wants to give them to us as the need arises.

- If we plan to employ someone to be part of the business engine, it is vital that we employ the right person— someone who wants to be part of a success story, who understands and passionately embraces the vision and business ethos.

Contact the Author

To contact Bryan Waters, please email him at:

bryan@businessingod.co.uk

Or visit his website at:

www.businessingod.co.uk

A new, exciting title from
DESTINY IMAGE™ EUROPE

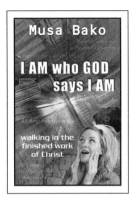

I AM WHO GOD SAYS I AM
Walking in the Finished Work of Christ
by Musa Bako

People come and go, but only a few people make a meaningful impact in their lifetime. Only a few people discover their purpose, turn it into passion, and fight for it like they do not have any other option. These are the people who reach greatness.

I Am Who God Says I Am was inspired as a tool to show you that you can achieve greatness in life and that there is no limitation before you.

Through the pages of this book you will discover:

- Why some prophecies and God's promises don't come to pass and how you can position yourself to see them fulfilled in you.

- How to keep your hopes alive in the midst of hopelessness and how to overcome discouragement.

- How to exercise your Kingdom authority and walk in victory over sickness, disease, failure, and fear.

- How to be filled with the fullness of God.

ISBN: 978-88-89127-94-0

Additional copies of this book and other book
titles from DESTINY IMAGE™ EUROPE
are available at your local bookstore.

We are adding new titles every month!

To view our complete catalog online, visit us at:
www.eurodestinyimage.com

Send a request for a catalog to:

Via della Scafa, 29/14
65013 Città Sant'Angelo (Pe), ITALY
Tel. +39 085 4716623 • +39 085 8670146
info@eurodestinyimage.com

"Changing the world, one book at a time."

Are you an author?

Do you have a "today" God-given message?

CONTACT US

We will be happy to review your manuscript
for the possibility of publication:

publisher@eurodestinyimage.com
http://www.eurodestinyimage.com/pages/AuthorsAppForm.htm